WITH THE
CORNWALL TERRITORIALS
ON THE WESTERN FRONT

BEING

THE HISTORY OF THE FIFTH BATTALION DUKE OF
CORNWALL'S LIGHT INFANTRY IN THE GREAT WAR

Compiled from official records and other sources

BY
E. C. MATTHEWS
Lieut. (retired), D.C.L.I., and
Lieut. Camb. Univ. Contingent O.T.C.
Author of "A Subaltern in the Field," etc

Illustrated by THE HON. J. R. L. FRENCH,

JOHN HASSALL, R.I., and others

With Maps by E. C. MATTHEWS, F.R.G.S.

AN INTRODUCTION
BY
BRIG.-GENERAL LORD ST LEVAN

The Naval & Military Press Ltd

❖

Reproduced by kind permission of the Central Library,
Royal Military Academy, Sandhurst

Published by

The Naval & Military Press Ltd

Unit 10, Ridgewood Industrial Park,

Uckfield, East Sussex,

TN22 5QE England

Tel: +44 (0) 1825 749494

Fax: +44 (0) 1825 765701

www.naval-military-press.com

© The Naval & Military Press Ltd 2004

Col. H.R.H. Edward, A. C. G. A. P. D., Prince of Wales, Duke of Cornwall,
K.G., G.C.M.G., G.C.V.O., G.B.E., M.C., W. Gds.

Photo by Bessano

Edward P 1919.

Dedication

WHAT dedication could be more fitting to this volume than to the memory of those who fell in action whilst serving their King and Country in the ranks of the 1/5th Battalion, Duke of Cornwall's Light Infantry, 1914-1918 ? To exemplify the spirit of sacrifice so typical of the traditional British hero, the following verses composed in a rest-camp near Ypres by the late Alan Crawhall Challoner, an Officer killed at Hooge whilst serving with the 6th Battalion, Duke of Cornwall's Light Infantry, are published :—

" If I were killed to-day, my chief regret,
　In this the greatest—worst of all the wars—
Would surely be that I my fate had met
　Without a chance of furthering the cause.

If I could put one bullet in a foe,
　Put just one German helmet in my kit,
Then, if I have to, I'm prepared to go,
　For, after all, I've done my little bit ! "

INTRODUCTION

INTRODUCTION

The Great War has been fought and won.

It remains to be seen if England knows how to make the best use of the experience she has gained.

To do so it is essential in the first place that she should remember—remember how great the crisis was and how it needed the uttermost determination of the nation in effort, courage, and sacrifice to enable victory to be achieved.

In these days of hurry and hustle, when great questions suddenly arise, mature, and have to be decided in far less time than used to be taken for their consideration, there is a danger of forgetting.

It is a good thing that memorials to those who served and died for the country are being erected throughout the land.

But it is necessary that the meaning of these monuments should be understood.

Not only are they tributes to the patriotism and devotion to duty of those whose names are inscribed on them, but they point out to us and to our successors the path of duty, which everyone who believes in British freedom must follow if he wishes to preserve that priceless heritage.

Now this book and those like it are valuable and necessary compliments to these memorials. They explain and illustrate their meaning.

This is the record of a territorial battalion which was practically raised afresh during the war from a population unaccustomed to military life, as was the case with many similar battalions at that time.

An account of what these men did and suffered is valuable to the country—and especially to Cornwall—and the County owes a great debt to Lieut. Matthews for having undertaken such a difficult task, and for the manner in which he has carried it out.

We read in this book of the difficulties of the early training, accentuated by some of the best instructors being called to serve at the front, and of the gradual emergence of a body of disciplined men, who did good service as soon as they joined the army in the field. First they were employed in the unobtrusive but hard and necessary work of a pioneer battalion, making and repairing roads and trenches, etc., and in consolidating military works of all kinds; and then, when called upon, showed that they could do their duty equally well in the firing line and earning the special distinction of being mentioned in dispatches for their conduct.

That conduct, as related in this book, speaks for itself, even without the commendation so freely expressed by the Officers under whose command the battalion served.

Some of the large sums of money we are spending on education might well be devoted to providing copies of this history to every school in the county, and every library and public institution should obtain them.

The Duke of Cornwall's Light Infantry is, and always has been, a famous regiment, of which the County may well be proud; and the record of the 1/5th Battalion in the Great War furnishes an example which Cornwall will expect future generations to follow should the occasion ever again arise.

I commend Lieut. Matthews' book to all Cornishmen.

St. Levan *Brig.-Genl.*

PREFACE

PREFACE

WHEN I first thought of writing the official history of my old Regiment in the Great War I shuddered. My mind carried me to great fields—France, Belgium, Italy, Palestine, and brought me back to crowded details—the still morning in the trenches, the wet miserable weather, and so on. But now, having accomplished a portion of the work, I can only throw myself on the good nature of my readers, and assure them that the self-imposed task has been a labour of real pleasure.

At the outset I met with much opposition and discouragement. Very few were interested at all in the History—most of us were sick and tired of anything connected with War—we wished to forget, and we were quite content to allow the mud and misery of those days to recede into the limbo of the past. But there were some to whom the suggestion of a History was sacred, and rightly so. The Roll of Honour of the Duke of Cornwall's Light Infantry alone justifies their emotion. I have no doubt but that those who read the " In Memoriam " columns in *The Times* find their minds wandering back to the old front line, the grey dawn of ' Zero ' hour, with the sight of those glittering, cold bayonets, the crouching figures, the dismal silence of that prelude, the forced laugh of old ' Tommy ' as he swallowed his last ration of rum, and lastly, the aftermath—' something accomplished, something done.'

Surely the memory of these things—these battles fought over once again—ought to have inspired us to pay a last tribute to our dead comrades by supporting this History. But it was not so. I trust that I am too true a patriot to allow my modesty to prevent plain speaking. The general response to my appeals for subscriptions to defray the cost of production, and contributions to build up the narrative, may be summed up in that word ' apathy.' Apart from a very few Officers of the old professional

Army and relatives of the fallen, there was not the slightest expression of that *esprit de corps* which for years before the war had served as the trade mark of every good Regiment. The net result was that I had to embark on my task almost single-handed.

Although I knew that to launch a book with an obvious limited circulation without substantial capital was a hazard, I really believed it could be done, and the Officers and men would rally around me. One or two of the senior Officers, with a lifelong association with the Regiment, were equally confident. But I must confess that my Publisher and many others with much experience on the troubled sea of ink, scoffed at the bare idea of success under the circumstances. I, on the other hand, disputed that they had taken into account that unknown factor— the spirit and the comradeship of the old Regiment ; and it was on this I staked everything, and I started.

My aim throughout this book has been to set down exactly what the ordinary unit did, and what the ordinary soldier thought, during those strenuous days in France and Flanders. Much has been included which the professional soldier would like to see deleted, but I think I am right in viewing the war as a people's war, and not as a purely professional war. I have endeavoured to clearly lay out for the professional soldier the tactical incidents of the campaign as far as the unit was concerned, but at the same time I have tried to be human, and to enlighten the mother who perhaps lost her only son, as to what he did and what he thought in action. To strike this happy medium has been no easy task.

I have to plead guilty in perhaps omitting some names of Officers, N.C.O.'s and men entitled to special mention. In all these cases their names and deeds have not been known to me, and generally their modesty has contributed towards the unfortunate omissions. Moreover, I sincerely think that most of us did, or might have done, equally as well as those who received honours or mentions under the circumstances.

To say that the man who won the V.C. is a hero, and the man who did not is not equally a hero, would be untrue and unfair. Many deeds which deserved recognition and mention now just remain in the memories of those who did them, and others have faded into oblivion.

My first intention was to bring out one volume which would cover the History of the whole Regiment. In order to gain a true impression of the History of the D.C.L.I., I thought it unwise to separate the 1914-1919 records from those of other wars. But as time passed, and I became more acquainted with the material at hand, I found this was impossible. The official records alone of one Battalion in the Great War baffled my original intention. Although to separate the records might lead to a false perspective, it would be useless to confuse the doings of the 1st Battalion in France and Italy with those of the 2nd Battalion in Macedonia. Moreover, the detail of the Great War is so crowded that it would be impossible to cram all the Battalion

Histories into one volume together with the records since the Regiment was formed.

The Regiment was raised in 1702 by Colonel Fox, and was known as Fox's Marines; it appears for the first few years of its experience to have done most of its fighting at sea, Colonel Fox being killed in action during the defence of Gibraltar in 1705. After eleven years of foreign service the Regiment was disbanded in 1713. It was, however, reinstated in March, 1715, and in consequence of gallant services, incorporated with Regiments of the Line as the 32nd Regiment of Foot, and allowed to rank from date of original formation. The Regiment seems to have served in the British Isles for some years, and in 1741 the 2nd Battalion D.C.L.I. was raised. Originally numbering the 57th Regiment, it afterwards became the 46th. Between 1742 and 1756 the Regiment saw a good deal of Foreign Service and became entitled to ' Dettingen ' on its Regimental Colours.

In 1756, on the renewal of war with France, a second Battalion of the 32nd Regiment was raised. It was numbered the 71st Regiment in 1758, but was disbanded in 1763.

In 1777 at the battle of Brandywine Creek in the American War of Independence the 46th Regiment earned the honourable distinction of " Red Feathers." The Light Company surprised and routed a superior force of American Rebels. The survivors of the American Force swore to be revenged. The 46th Light Company hearing of this, sent word to the enemy that to prevent any other Regiment from being taken for them they would dye their white pom-poms red. This they did, and this episode is the origin of the red pagri worn on the white helmet by the Regiment, of the red plume worn in the khaki helmet on foreign service, and also of the red ground to the cap badge.

In 1782 county titles were conferred, the 32nd becoming " Cornwall Regiment," and the 67th " South Devonshire Regiment." From 1782 till 1805 was a time of comparative peace ; but in 1808 the 46th Regiment earned the honour " Dominica " for exemplary valour in the defence of the Island of that name against a very superior French Force, and in the troublous times which so soon followed the 32nd earned the following honours :—1809, Corunna ; 1812, Salamanca ; 1813, Pyrennes, Nivelle, Nive ; 1814, Orthes, and finally 1815, Waterloo.

From 1815, when all nations were more or less exhausted and resting after the Wars of Napoleon, until 1847, there is nothing of particular interest to record ; but in 1848-49 the 32nd, who were in India, earned the honours of Goojerat and Mooltan ; and in 1854 the 46th earned the honour Sevastopol.

The awful days of the Indian Mutiny soon followed. Not only did the 32nd lose a heavy toll of officers and men, but the records of the Regiment show that 47 women and 55 children also perished ; and in the defence of Lucknow it is recorded that between the 31st May and 22nd November, excluding women and children,

15 officers and 364 other ranks were killed, and 11 officers and 198 other ranks wounded. In 1858 the Regiment was made " Light Infantry," in consideration of the enduring gallantry displayed in the defence of the Residency of Lucknow.

In 1877 the 32nd L.I., and 46th Foot became linked Battalions, and later, in 1881, when the Territorial system was introduced, the 32nd L.I., 46th Foot, and Royal Cornwall Rangers Militia, became respectively the 1st, 2nd and 3rd Battalions of the Duke of Cornwall's Light Infantry. In 1882 the 2nd Battalion earned the honours Egypt, 1882, and Tel-el-kebir, and again were on active service in 1885 in Egypt, where Nile, 1884-85, was added. In later years the 1st Battalion saw service with the Tirah Expeditionary Force on the Indian Frontier ; and the 2nd Battalion served throughout the South African War, becoming entitled to add South Africa and Paardeberg to its honours.

At the outbreak of the Great War, the D.C.L.I. consisted of two Regular Battalions (of which the first was stationed in Ireland and the second in Hong-Kong), the Special Reserve Battalion (the 3rd), and two Territorial Battalions (the 4th and 5th). The Devon and Cornwall Infantry Brigade was in camp at Exmouth—the 5th Battalion D.C.L.I. being at this time (August 4th, 1914) under the command of Colonel Jerome.

On receipt of mobilization orders the Battalion at once moved to Falmouth, its war station. Here, with the 4th Battalion D.C.L.I., it provided the garrisons for the forts at Pendennis and St. Anthony, and also for the large number of German liners and sailing vessels which our Fleet had collected from the " Narrow Seas," the Mediterranean and Atlantic, and convoyed for safe custody to Falmouth Harbour, just in the same way that hundreds of years previously our men-of-war had driven most of the Dutch Mercantile Marine into the Thames. Falmouth was at that time a very interesting place, thronged with visitors who had come down to see the captured German shipping. Whilst at Falmouth the Battalion was brought up to full strength by the addition of the Territorial and National Reserve, and here it remained until the end of August, when it entrained for Salisbury Plain, going under canvas at Perham Down Camp, Ludgershall.

The early doings of most battalions so far as this war is concerned, and especially during the early stages of training at home, resemble one another so closely, that to give a history of one battalion is but to repeat the history already written regarding others. So it is not the intention to deal at any length with the period when the break of war found this Territorial Reserve Battalion, in common with many others, engaged in its annual training, but will rather, passing by these minor events, go on to deal with the more exciting incidents during the war, and the methods by which the training so carefully carried out at home, was successfully put into practice in France and Flanders.

One incident of training deserves singular note. The battalion was fully occupied, especially in furnishing Guards for military works, etc., at Avonmouth, Leithfield, Coventry and Farnboro'. The detachment at Farnboro' was ordered to guard the Royal Aircraft Factory, and while so employed one of the sentries held up a motor car, the occupant of which claimed to be no less a personage than the Prime Minister himself. "Don't care if you be the King of England. You baint be going to pass me without a pass," retorted the sentry.

During the month of October a large number of the 5th D.C.L.I. volunteered for foreign service with the 4th Battalion, and were accordingly transferred to that unit. The remainder of the battalion returned to Cornwall to be billeted on the people of Bodmin. A move was made to Newquay later, where a fortnight was spent before the battalion proceeded to Newcastle-on-Tyne in order to undertake coast defence duties. The troops were billeted in Cramlington, a typical

North-country village, situated in bleak country, and surrounded by coal pits, black pit heaps, and numerous stacks belching forth volumes of smoke.

The battalion, now under the command of Lieut.-Colonel Pleydell-Bouverie, at once set to work on the construction of the 2nd and 3rd lines of the North-East coast defences, digging and wiring, etc. The month of December witnessed a call for volunteers for service abroad with the 6th Devons, and 60 other ranks at once volunteered and were transferred to this unit. At the same time the men of the National Reserve were recalled for guard duties in Cornwall. During the same month also, Major Bawden and N.C.O. Instructors were returned to Bodmin Depot (T.F.) for the purpose of recruiting and training reinforcements for the battalion. The remainder of the battalion undertook a spell of heavy training under active service conditions, including " stand to " one hour before dawn, sometimes in two feet of snow, followed by a full day's digging and wiring along the coast.

In January, 1915, four company organisation was introduced, and " A," " B," " C " and " D " Companies were placed respectively under the command of Captains M. Stewart, Walters, M. F. Edyvean, and F. Williams. About this time Colonel N. Gray, T.D., took over command of the battalion from Lieut.-Colonel Pleydell-Bouverie.

Towards the end of March, Lieut.-Colonel Parker succeeded Colonel Gray in command of the battalion, and the Adjutant, Captain Mander, was attached to H.Q. Home Garrison Company, Lieutenant Tyacke now acting as Adjutant. The battalion moved on April 14th to Cambois, camping about 400 yards from Cambois Colliery Pit. Whilst stationed at this place, Zeppelins several times flew overhead, but passed on to drop their bombs on towns in the surrounding district. The usual training was carried on at Cambois, and during the first week in August the battalion was relieved by the 21st Provisional Battalion of the Northumberland Fusiliers.

On August 14th, Colonel Parker left for Tavistock to take command of the 2/5th Battalion D.C.L.I., and Major Bawden assumed command of the 1/5th. It was the popular opinion that the D.C.L.I. had been moved to the North through a clerical error on the part of the War Office, who were supposed to have read D.C.L.I. for D.L.I.

Orders were received for the battalion to proceed to Falmouth for the purpose of recruiting and completing training for overseas. It detrained at Falmouth on August 31st—the battalion at this time possessing only two Maxim guns and twenty spring Bayonets. The period from September to the end of the year was spent under canvas at Trevethan Camp, but a move was made to near the Castle on the 6th October, and to St. Anthony on 6th December, where the battalion stayed until moving to Perham Down on 14th April, 1916. On May 5th, it were inspected by His Majesty the King on Bulford Plains, and the following day moved to Jellalabad Barracks, Tidworth. Here pioneer and divisional training was carried on until May 20th, when orders to pack up, prior to embarking for France, were received.

What followed I have endeavoured to put forward as a plain story in simple language, but before unveiling the part played by the 1/5th Battalion in the struggles on the Western Front, justice demands that something be said about the Reserve Battalion at home, which was continually supplying drafts to the parent Battalion overseas. The 5th Battalion ultimately became the 1/5th D.C.L.I., and when in Northumberland in the early days of 1915, Major C. E. Whitford was sent to Bodmin in order to raise the 2/5th. The latter Battalion was first raised for the purpose of sending drafts to the 1/5th abroad.

About May, 1915, the 2/5th D.C.L.I. proceeded to camp at Whitchurch Down, near Tavistock, with the remainder of a Brigade composed of the 3/4th D.C.L.I., and the Devons. Lieut.-Colonel W. F. Parker was in command of the 2/5th, with Major C. E. Whitford, as Second-in-Command, and Captain C. N. W. Tyacke as Adjutant. Here on the fringe of that bleak Dartmoor training was carried out, and many Officers under this formation found their way later into other Battalions of the Regiment, and other Regiments or Corps. Mention must be made of Alex George Jermyn Alderson, who was formerly a Master at Sherbourne. He was unfortunately killed in England during bombing practice with the Machine Gun Corps on the 19th October, 1916. Alderson was at Oxford, and took Holy Orders, before proceeding to Sherbourne.

From Tavistock the Battalion went to Exmouth, and from thence to Boscombe, Bournemouth. At Hursley Park, near Winchester, the 2/5th became amalgamated with the 3/4th under the title of the 4th Reserve Battalion, D.C.L.I. Lieut.-Colonel W. F. Parker, who formerly commanded the 1/5th, became Commanding Officer.

After being at Sutton Veney and other places, the 4th Reserve Battalion proceeded to Ireland.

After the war ended, it was the desire of Lieut.-Colonel E. B. Ward, D.S.O., who commanded the 1/5th Battalion, that a short history should be written to perpetuate the memory of the Battalion and its work. The direct outcome was a little book arranged by A. D. Chegwin, entitled *War Services of the 1/5th Battalion, Duke of Cornwall's Light Infantry*. In expressing my appreciation of Lieutenant Chegwin's industry, I have to acknowledge that his account forms the skeleton of the present work.

On behalf of my Regiment I have to thank H.R.H. the Prince of Wales, as Colonel-in-Chief of the Duke of Cornwall's Light Infantry, for his kindness in sending his autographed photograph for inclusion in the History.

The Introduction to this volume has been written by Brig.-General Lord St. Levan, whose interest in the Cornwall County Regiment is known to all. Captain the Hon. J. R. L. French, and Mr. John Hassall, R.I., I also thank for their praiseworthy efforts.

Amongst others who have so kindly assisted me by placing various facts and documents at my disposal, one name stands out in golden letters. I refer to Lieut. A. Leonard Poole, of Clare College, Cambridge, for whose untiring kindness I cannot offer sufficient thanks. I might well relinquish any claim of precedence and introduce him as collaborator.

I am indebted to Brig.-General T. E. Edmonds, and others, of the Historical Section (Military Branch), Committee of Imperial Defence, for allowing me facilities to consult the War Diaries. Captain G. K. Rose, M.C., has kindly consented to my quoting from his "Story of the 2/4th Oxfordshire and Buckinghamshire Light Infantry." Colonel William Capper, Miss C. Briggs, Mr. E. Haylock, O.B.E., and Mr. |H. C. Dickens, O.B.E., I have to thank for a number of details ;

and Captain John Trehane, M.C., I am grateful to for lending me some valuable maps.

Lastly, it would be unkind not to acknowledge the help and interest of the Publisher and Printer whilst the work was passing through the Press. They have done all that is in their power, apart from commercial interests, to make the History a success.

Despite the energy and resource without which this book would never have found birth, I feel that I am conferring an honour on myself in being associated even in so modest a way with one of the twelve Battalions in the whole British Army mentioned by itself in despatches. That the records after such distinction are worthy of being produced and preserved in Press publication form need not be questioned. The glorious traditions of the old ' Dukes ' have more than been maintained, and it is with a feeling of dread that I may have failed to find words great enough to do justice to the many gallant deeds which the Regiment has to its credit.

In the event of a second edition of this volume being published in the future, readers are invited to submit proposals for alterations, additions and corrections to this edition. This especially refers to data, etc., and such communications may be directed to the Compiler or Publisher at the addresses to be found in the pages of this History.

There are some words throughout this volume which may be unfamiliar to those who were lucky enough to escape the life of the trench-dweller in France and Belgium, 1914-18. I have purposely included these words of "trench language," and I think it is well that they should remain. Such words as "scrounger," "pip-squeak," "stunt" "wind-up," convey meanings much more vivid than any which the classical dictionaries might give us.

The thin, long line of khaki no longer tapers across the lowlands of Flanders, the plains of Artois or the hills of Picardy, but a thin, long line of wooden crosses still peep above the horizon of those regions. They point the way, like stepping-stones, to the tragedy of that ' nine days' wonder.'   The pilgrim beholds . . . . . ponders . . . . and as he turns and gazes at the splendour of the setting sun, the echoes of his thoughts come back from afar with the question " Was man created mad ? "

SOCIETY OF ARMY
       HISTORICAL RESEARCH,
   R. U. S. I.,
       WHITEHALL, S.W.1.
August, 1921.   E. C. MATTHEWS.

CONTENTS

LIST OF ILLUSTRATIONS

MAPS

For ever rolling forth their tale of hate,
The giant guns, dark harbingers of death,
What know they of the misery they bring
To those whom conscience, or their Country's King,
Has called to battle? Can they feel
The evil that lives after them, their mission done,
Or know compassion for the victims of their wrath
So quickly risen? Or, is it that they know not Life,
That pleasant life so dear to mortals—Nay,
They must be soulless that could take away
The mind that gave them being, from its resting place.
But though they batter, yet they cannot overcome
The courage born of Empire, and the Pride
Of the unconquered race, whose fighting fame
Is known in every land. Guns with guns
And men with men shall close. Then shall they know
That England's name is Victory—in that hour
Shall they repent them that they strove
To cage the Lion, whose cage no man can fashion.

Verses from the Front (Ypres), February, 1916,
by the late Major J. E. P. Rae, 7th Batt. D.C.L.I.

LAVENTIE,
MAY TO SEPTEMBER,
1916

CHAPTER I

Laventie, May to September, 1916

The 1/5th D.C.L.I. lands in France. On the 21st May, 1916, about which date the British Forces in the Field were making silent but colossal preparations for the great Battles of the Somme, the 1/5th D.C.L.I., comprising 34 Officers and 998 other ranks, embarked at Southampton for France. It was a surprise to many who stepped aboard the transport that prospects of real active service were at last taking definite shape. Frequent rumours of 48 hours' notice to proceed overseas had been entertained, but as time passed without developments beliefs in rumours eventually became rare.

A Cornish Battalion composed of Cornishmen. After a smooth passage across the Channel, the Battalion disembarked at Le Havre, and was accommodated under canvass in No. 2 Camp, Sanvic, away on the heights overlooking the seaport town. It is interesting to note that unlike many Battalions which consisted of a mixture of Scotchmen, Welshmen and Irishmen, the majority of the 1/5th D.C.L.I. were men from the County. To be exact 948 Cornishmen crossed over on that day. They were commanded by Lieut.-Colonel W. A. Bawden.

Several days later, after a usual troop train journey up to the line, the Battalion detrained at Merville, a pleasant little town which, however, suffered much from shell-fire later in the war. Pioneer training was commenced on the 25th of May under the orders of the 61st Division to which the Battalion belonged. The portion of the Western Front which received some of the spade-work of the Cornishmen was that in front of Laventie, just north of Neuve Chapelle, which was then considered a fairly quiet part of the line. Not that any part of the line was really quiet, but there was usually nothing to report beyond spasms of shell-fire, raids and reconnaissances. And these, are far from inviting to anyone who knows what they mean.

Shortly after the arrival of the 61st Division in the Merville area, the Welsh Division then holding the line was relieved, and the 61st took rein. Subsequently much instruction and useful information had been gained in pioneer work

THE CORNISH ARMS AND MOTTO "ONE AND ALL."

The Cornish Arms and motto "One and All," are supposed to have originated during the time of the Crusaders. The story is, that a Duke of Cornwall was taken prisoner by the Saracens and held to ransom for fifteen bezants; on the news reaching Cornwall, the whole of the population subscribed. The fifteen bezants are represented by fifteen balls in the shield of the Cornish Arms, with the motto "One and All," meaning, it is presumed, that all subscribed.

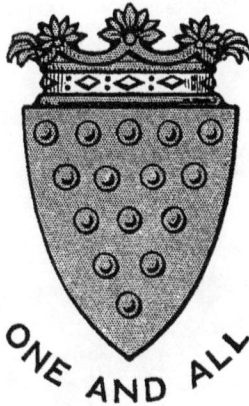

Drawn by
THE HON. J. R. L. FRENCH.

by the Cornwalls through attachment to other units.

First Casualties, and the First Honour Won.
Captain E. M. Hodson was appointed Acting Adjutant, and 2nd Lieut. J. McNally, Acting Quartermaster, and the Battalion suffered its first casualties in the early days of June. About this time also Private Stevens, a native of Nanstallon, near Bodmin, won for the Battalion its first honour in the war. He received the Military Medal for bravely and unhesitatingly walking over the top of the parapet into " No-Man's-Land " under heavy enemy machine-gun fire, and extricating from a pile of *debris* an infantryman who had been buried by a shell explosion. Private Stevens got his burden safely back to the trench, but unfortunately he himself was killed in action on July 17th—about six weeks later.

The first effects of shell-fire having been left behind gave the Cornishmen an opportunity of settling down to their active service rôle. When we remember that this Territorial Battalion was recruited mostly from a peaceful country type of man, it is to the credit of those concerned that they stood their ground so well—especially in the crucible of such a fierce war as this. It is good to think that in Field General Courts-martial held for the trial of soldiers deserting His Majesty's Forces in face of the enemy, mercy was liberally extended, consistent with, of course, the safety and welfare of the whole Army. Most of the men at this period of the war were volunteers drawn from all classes—students, clerks, farm labourers—and whose trial of nerves before never exceeded that of a boxing contest. It would be libel to brand every man a coward who suddenly obeyed the demands of his natural instincts during intense shelling.

Appreciation of Work from Corps and Division. Nothing of importance happened to the Battalion, and the remainder of the month of June was employed in the usual pioneer work. There were the constant fatigues—the revetting, sand-bagging, digging, and so on. Pioneers were always in demand, and from every part of the Divisional front the 1/5th D.C.L.I. would be seen like ants for ever busy in repairing, constructing and carrying. It would be difficult to enumerate all the duties of a Pioneer Battalion, or to allow full justice to those who shared the work, but it is pleasing to know that, now and again, congratulations poured in from Corps and Divisional Headquarters. During all these periods of activity the Cornwalls suffered the usual casualties which brought reinforcements from the base at Rouen.

19*th July*.* On the 27th June the G.O.C. 61st Division sent word that he had made a special note of the able and gallant work of the Cornwall Pioneers in connection with the recent sapping operations carried out. Onward until July 19th events were eclipsed by operations farther South, but on the latter date the 61st Division made an attack which was shared by the 5th Australian holding trenches further north. Captain G. K. Rose, M.C., in his vivid story of the 2/4th Oxfordshire and Buckinghamshire Light Infantry describes the action thus :—" . . . . the comparative deadlock in the Somme fighting rendered necessary vigorous measures against the enemy elsewhere on the

* The attack at Fromelles, on the Aubers Ridge, was subsidiary to the Battle of Bazentin Ridge in the Somme operations when Longueval, Trones Wood and Ovillers were tactically captured, and the subsequent attacks on High Wood were made. The limits of the Fromelles action were Road Aubers—Fauquissart—Laventie—Rouge-de-Bout—Fleurbaix (exclusive)—la Boutillerie—Bas Maisnil. These names are geographical, but who is likely to forget such bye-ways as ' Lonely Erith,' ' Rotten Row,' ' Bodmin Trench,' or ' Bond Street,' which no longer echo with the tinkling of mess-tins, scabbards and rifles, or the heavy tramp of an exhausted fatigue party ?

front.   A gas attack from the Fauquissart sector
was planned but never carried out.   Trench
mortars and rifle grenades were continuously
employed to make life as unpleasant as possible
for the enemy, whose trenches soon became, to
all appearances, a rubbish heap.   All day and
much of the night the ' mediums ' fell in and
about the German trenches and . . . . . this
harassing warfare had a crisis in July.   The
operations . . . . . . were designed as a demon-
stration to assist our attack upon the Somme
and to hold opposite to the XI Corps certain
German reserves, which, it was feared, would
entrain at Lille and be sent south.   That object
was achieved, but at the cost of severe casualties
to the divisions engaged, which were launched
in daylight after artillery preparation, which
results proved to have been inadequate, against
a trench-system strongly manned and garrisoned
by very numerous machine-guns.   The objectives
assigned to the 61st Division were not captured,
while the Australians further north, after entering
the German trenches and taking prisoners, though
they held on tenaciously under heavy counter-
attacks, were eventually forced to withdraw.
' The staff work,' said the farewell message from
the XI Corps to the 61st Division three months

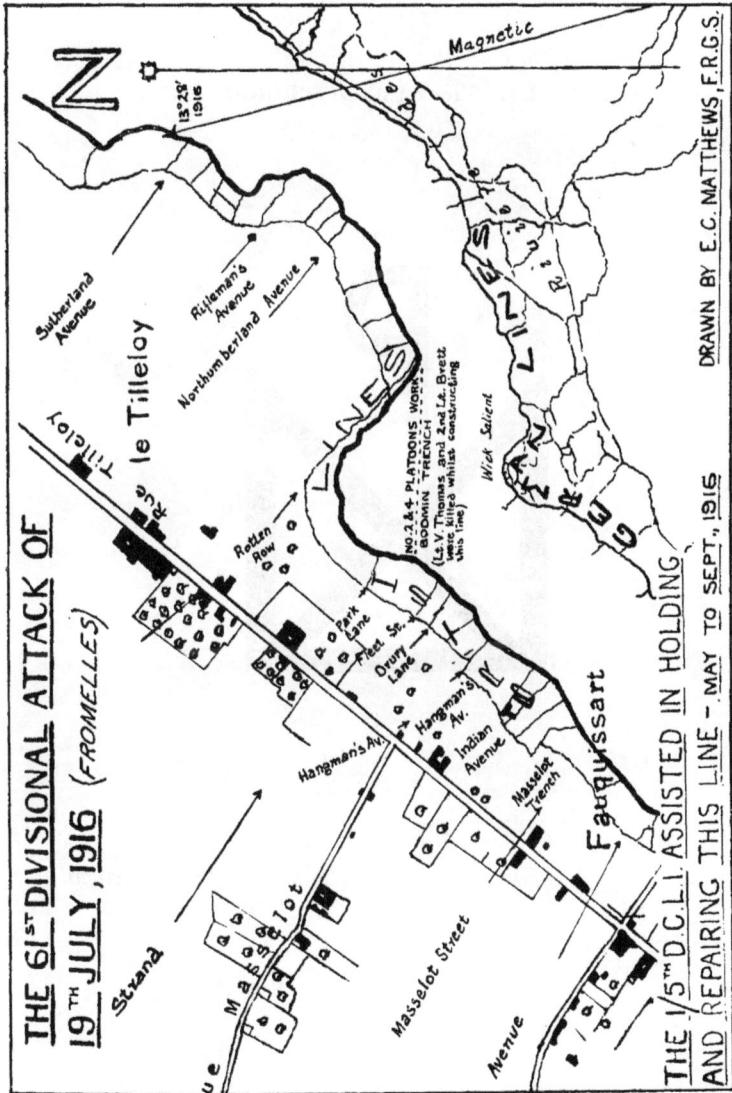

THE 61ST DIVISIONAL ATTACK OF 19TH JULY, 1916 (FROMELLES)

THE 1/5TH D.C.L.I. ASSISTED IN HOLDING AND REPAIRING THIS LINE - MAY TO SEPT., 1916

DRAWN BY E.C. MATTHEWS, F.R.G.S.

Magnetic

13°23' 1916

Sutherland Avenue

Rifleman's Avenue

le Tilleloy

Northumberland Avenue

Wick Salient

Robin Row

Rue Tilleloy

No. 2 & 4 PLATOONS WORK BODMIN TRENCH
(Lt. V. Thomas and 2nd Lt. Brett were killed whilst constructing this line)

Park Lane

Fleet St.

Drury Lane

Hangman's Av.

Indian Avenue

Masselot Trench

Fauquissart

Hangman's Av.

Strand

Rue Masselot

Masselot Street

Avenue

To face page 7)

1/5TH D.C.L.I. (PIONEERS) DIVISIONAL SIGN.

Drawn by
CAPT. THE HON. J. R. L. FRENCH.

later, ' for these operations was excellent.' Men
and officers alike did their utmost to make the
attack of July 19th a success, and it behoves all
to remember the sacrifice of those who fell with
appropriate gratitude. It was probably the last
occasion on which large parties of storming
infantry were sent forward through ' sally
ports.' . . . . . . After the operations of July
19th the former methods of trench warfare were
resumed. The Division's casualties in the attack
had been over 2,000, and time was required to
reorganise and make up these losses."

A short time afterwards, two Platoons of the
1/5th D.C.L.I. were dispatched to the 93rd
Brigade front for Pioneer work, and following
this, a letter was received from Brig.-General
J. D. Ingles, commanding the 93rd Brigade, who
wrote :—" Please accept on my own behalf and
also on that of the 93rd Brigade, our sincere
thanks for the invaluable assistance given to us
by the officers and men of the two Platoons you
so kindly lent to us to help repair damage done
to our line on the night of 27th and 28th July.
The amount and quality of the work done could
not have been improved upon, and is a fine
example of what can be done."

During the month of August nothing happened out of the ordinary.   2nd Lieut. E. H. W. Brett was admitted into Hospital on the 1st, having been wounded in the head by a sniper, and the next day news came through that he had died in the 1/2nd London Clearing Station.   He was buried in the cemetery near by.   There were the usual reliefs, and hardly noticeable was the silent influx of officers and men from the Base, joining and re-joining.   They were quickly absorbed into the Battalion, and through them news of England leaked to many an anxious ear. Offtimes one of these arrivals would bring ' confidential reports ' of what was going to happen, and which was stated to be known only to a second person beside Haig himself.   Hindenburg was believed to have something up both his sleeves, and so on.   But after a time it was with evident satisfaction that experienced Tommy would retort " Yo' can't tell a' old Soldier anythink."

2nd Lieutenant F. W. Yelf was wounded on the 1st September, and during the month some men were sent to the Infantry base depot at Rouen, having been found permanently unfit for duty in advanced areas.   A few were discovered to be under-age, and were accordingly sent down the line.

At Laventie on the 16th September, the day was considered a holiday, having been granted by the G.O.C., 61st Division. Needless to add it was utilised for the purpose of holding a day's programme of athletic sports in conjunction with the R.E.'s. At 6.30 in the evening, however, " B " Company, consisting of 4 Officers and 172 other ranks proceeded on detachment owing to an extension of Divisional front, and the two Platoons of " A " Company under Lieut. J. Trehane and 2nd Lieut. P. Morcom, remained in the trenches another four days.

On the 22nd September, the Battalion suffered the loss of Lieut. F. B. V. Thomas, of " A " Company, who was killed in action by a sniper. He was buried at Laventie cemetery.

Meanwhile the gigantic struggle in Picardy was raging hot, and it was evident that sooner or later, the 61st Division would be swung into the furnace. Orders to move at last arrived as expected, and it was with real regret that most of the troops said " Good-bye " to old Laventie. Some happy days were spent there, and in looking forward many had unpleasant visions of that fuming cauldron of the Somme which for months had cruelly swallowed up the pick of our Army.

THE SOMME, OCTOBER, 1916,
TO MAY, 1917

CHAPTER II

The Somme, and the Advance to the Hindenburg Line, October, 1916 to May, 1917

On the 28th October the Battalion commenced marching to the Somme, and the day previous was spent in cleaning up billets preparatory to moving back from the Laventie front. Whilst at St. Floris, where the troops occupied billets, the usual instructional parades were carried out, and on November 2nd the Battalion continued trekking southwards, being billeted at villages and hamlets on the way. These halts were very pleasant, and ofttimes it was hard to realise there was a war on.

On the 10th there was an inspection of pioneer work by the G.O.C. 61st Division, and five days later the Battalion reached Beaumetz, from which motor buses and char-a-bancs conveyed it to hutments in Martinsart Wood, near Aveluy. November 17th found the 1/5th D.C.L.I. marching to dug-outs between Contalmaison and Posieres, and later it was attached to the 4th Canadian Division for pioneer work, during which several casualties were sustained. There were indeed casualties almost every night, Lieut. J. D. H. Maddrell being killed and Captain T. A. V. Wood severely wounded.

Whilst attached to the R.E.'s of the Canadian Division, the Pioneers were required to go up to the line each night, and assist in wiring and trench digging, etc. The Division was consolidating some gains in the region of Regina and Desire trenches. The famous Sausage Valley on the Somme at this time was not at all consoling. The billets were for the most part huge shell holes which had been made square and covered with corrugated iron or waterproof sheets. Most of the dug-outs were several inches deep in water and mud. Guns of all description surrounded the camp, mostly naval long-range and howitzers, which kept up an incessant firing day and night.

Aveluy. Due to the remainder of the 61st Division arriving in the area, the Battalion left Sausage Valley for some huts named Marlborough Huts, near the village of Aveluy, about four kilos east of Albert. These huts were a distinct improvement to the bivouacs of the Valley, for most of them contained stoves.

The Battalion now began to work with its own Division, for which it was very thankful,

and, although the Canadian rations were liberal
(including the rum), the men never favoured
being attached to strange Divisions. There was
an amusing story told about the Canadians.
A Canadian Colonel, having heard that an English
General of considerable reputation was to inspect
his men, harrangued them before the event,
concluding : " Now, boys, I count on you to do
me credit. Stand straight, keep your chins up,
don't spit, and for God's sake don't call me Alf."

The work of the Battalion consisted of revetting
existing trenches with brushwood hurdles. The
latter were carted to ' Tullock's Corner ' by the
regimental transport and ' man-handled ' onward,
or conveyed by the light railway—if intact, which
was not usually the case. In the story of the
2/4th Oxford and Bucks. Light Infantry, it
states : " . . . The British advance having reached
a standstill, the enemy's artillery was now firing
from more forward positions, and paid much
attention to places like Mouquet Farm, Tullock's
Corner, Zollern Redoubt, and Field Trench.
Parties of D.C.L.I. were daily at work upon the
latter, duckboarding and revetting, and completed a fine pioneers' job right up to Hessian.
Field Trench ranked among the best performances

of the Cornwalls, whose work altogether at this time deserved high praise."

" D " Company of the Cornwalls had the job of making new dug-outs, deep ones, in Hessian Trench, which necessitated continuous work being carried out by ' shifts.' The most difficult problem was not the task itself, but finding out where the work was actually located.   There were no conspicuous landmarks anywhere, and it was usually difficult for the Officer-in-charge of the working party to discover the location of his work in daylight. At night this was quite impossible without guides. Even the guides were never infallible on this point. On one occasion two Officers and a party of men of " D " Company set out to construct deep dug-outs in Hessian trench. Having followed a white tape to the end of the communication trench to Lancashire trench, they found their work easily, and decided that the return journey at nightfall would be equally simple. But it was not so. During the day someone had decided it wise to lay another white tape a short distance away from the original, and owing to the returning party having scattered by a 5.9 straffe that night, the group divided into two—one Officer, with a portion of his men, followed one white tape, and the other the second

ROUGH MAP SHOWING TRENCH SYSTEM ON THE SOMME, 1916

(To face page 17)

LIEUT.-COL. W. A. BAWDEN.

tape. It was only after a great deal of wandering that the portions of the party rejoined. In fact, each half turned up simultaneously in the Reserve Line (Zollern Trench) where a minor casualty was attended to. 2nd Lieut. F. Soward received a slight wound during the shelling, which caused a break up of his party.

Carus-Wilson takes command. The end of the month witnessed a number of casualties and a corresponding number of arrivals from the Base. Lieut.-Colonel W. A. Bawden relinquished command of the Battalion, and Major T. Carus-Wilson assumed responsibility of C.O. Lieut. A. J. F. Bawden returned to the Battalion for duty after having spent some months on a Staff course at 61st Divisional H.Q. He was posted as 2nd-in-command of " D " Company, and commanded that company during the absence of Captain Williams who attended the 5th Army Senior Officers' course.

Aveluy huts received greetings from German long-range guns from time to time, with some disastrous results to the horse lines, but about Christmas the Transport was singularly free from shelling. E

Christmas,
1916.

The band deteimined to remind the Battalion of the end of the old year, and the players were equally determined not to allow their throats to get dry, for they set out to play Christmas carols and hymns outside each Company Officers' Mess. The playing, with all due respects to the Bandmaster, was not a success, and the noise made by the band towards the end of its pilgrimage can best be imagined. A few luxuries were secured from the B.E.F. Canteens at Albert, and the superstitious inhabitants of that town were not backward in prophesying that when the overhanging Virgin of their church (the famous Albert Cathedral) fell, the war would cease. But, unfortunately, like a few other prophesies as to the duration of the war, it was doomed to absurdity. The overhanging Virgin fell, but the thunder-clouds still continued to roll, and so the prophecy was out-timed.

The ordinary pioneer work was resumed until after Christmas, when " D " Company was detailed to work on the road leading from Aveluy to Thiepval (Nab Road). " B " Company revetted the whole of the Field trench, a communication trench leading to Regina trench, with brushwood hurdles, while " A " and " C "

Companies laid duck-board tracks overland from various places.

2nd Lieut. A. H. Paull, Transport Officer, returned from leave on January 3rd, and three days later Lieut. J. Trehane was wounded in action. About this time Major R. C. F. Edyvean assumed 2nd-in-command of the Battalion, having relinquished command of " B " Company on Major Carus-Wilson's promotion. Captain E. M. Hodson took over " B " Company. The other Officers commanding companies were :—

" A " Company : Captain Thomas.
" B "   ,,   Captain E. M. Hodson.
" C "   ,,   Captain B. S. Hodge.
" D "   ,,   Captain F. Williams.

2nd Lieut. L. Smith joined the Battalion from 4th Reserve D.C.L.I. on 21st January, and was accordingly posted to " A " Company.

Lieut.-Colonel Carus-Wilson returned from ten days' leave on 30th January, and resumed his active interest in the work of the Battalion. No matter how far forward the Pioneer work happened to be, or however dangerous the position, a Subaltern in charge of a working party could always depend that the Colonel would turn up sometime during the day.

On Saturday, 3rd February, in the middle of a really enjoyable concert organised by the Padre, the Rev. J. Milum, rumours of a move to a village somewhere near Abbeville were circulated. Later the rumours developed into definite orders for the Battalion to proceed by train to Longpre, and the next morning the move commenced. The Battalion entrained, and the Transport went by road, making a three days' journey, which was quite pleasant though bitterly cold.

Training was resumed and sports indulged in at Longpre, and a few fortunate individuals found their way into Abbeville. This was only the second time that the Battalion had been far away from the line since its arrival on French soil in May, 1916. But, alas! it did not last long. Orders were received on Sunday, 11th February, for a move the following day back to the line, but to a point farther south than before. At this time the British were taking over a portion of the line south of the Somme from the French, and the 61st was one of the Divisions selected for this relief.

It was arranged that the Pioneers should wait at a place named Guillaucourt until the Infantry had relieved the French in the line. The Battalion proceeded, partly by train and partly by foot, arriving at Guillaucourt to meet the Transport which again had travelled by road.

Reorganisation of the Battalion. The Battalion was reorganised whilst lying in the neighbourhood of Guillaucourt, and a draft from home was posted in the various companies. Guillaucourt was not entirely a disagreeable place. There were still some excellent houses which were converted into billets. The Transport had good standings in an old brickworks, which was certainly a relief after the wretched standings on the Somme further north.

Later, the Battalion moved forward and occupied a rather scattered area in the region of Herleville, a village completely smashed up. Battalion Headquarters and "D" Company occupied the remnants of the village, or rather dug-outs in the village, and "A" and "B" Companies were in dug-outs about a mile further forward. "C" Company had a special job connected with a Light Railway in that area. If Herleville was ever famous for anything, it must have been rats. There were millions of them, and they possessed such powers of assimilation that boots, valise straps, and clothing soon disappeared with comparative ease.

In this new area the Companies were given distinct tasks. " C " Company had the duty of constructing a light railway as mentioned. " D " Company had the Herleville-Rosiere road to repair, but on the 9th February it was ordered to march southward, to join the 32nd Division, and act as Pioneers, whilst the 32nd Divisional Pioneers were away constructing railways.

Three Divisions held this sector of the line taken over from the French. They were the 61st, 35th and 32nd. The 32nd Division were on the extreme right of the British Army, and joined with the French across the Amiens-Roye road, east of the village of Le-Quesnoy which was then about a mile within our lines. Whilst here, Private C. Lawer, of " A " Company, was awarded the Military Medal for his gallant action of February 23rd. " Three men of ' A ' Company were adjusting a pump-hose on the parapet of Serpentine communication trench, when they struck a French hand-grenade which commenced to smoke. Lawer immediately picked it up and threw it into a shell-hole, where it exploded."

It was generally thought that the Germans would retire from the whole of the Somme area, working back towards St. Quentin. But at the same time it was hoped that an attack in the

32nd Divisional sector might convert this retirement into a retreat.   It was therefore planned that the French should attack across the 32nd Divisional front, and the show was organised for March 17th.   After the first attack by the French, the 32nd Division was detailed to follow up and take over their objectives, allowing the French to fall back.

The German retirement. The fateful morning arrived, and at zero-hour the French attacked . . . only to discover that the Germans had already commenced their retirement.

It was clear that the German lines had been very thinly held for some days.   A small number of the enemy apparently tenanted the front line for the purpose of firing fixed-rifles, and sending up illuminating rockets during the night. This clever ruse was very successful, as it gave our troops the impression that the line was held in force.   It was some time before the Allies again succeeded in getting into touch with the enemy.

Roads had been carefully mined, and booby traps abounded, but otherwise everything was uneventful, and the retirement was followed up quite peaceably.   The Pioneers had the task of repairing roads and filling in craters caused by mines, and in looking back to that period many have regarded it as the most satisfactory one spent by the Battalion in France.

Matigny.   At last Matigny was reached, and there the Battalion remained for some time. These " rest days " were full of training in Platoon and Company drill, the Lewis gun and Bombing, but there was no active warfare—no shelling or bombing, although occasionally one could hear the dismal gun-fire some miles away.

It was from Matigny that the Adjutant was invalided home, only to die in a London hospital twelve months later. Captain Ball was a regular soldier beginning his career in the Guards, but was gazetted to the Royal Fusiliers during the war. He was appointed Adjutant to the 1/5th D.C.L.I. before the Battalion went overseas, and continued in this capacity until May, 1917.

" D " Company had several casualties at Matigny owing to a wall falling on to a cellar roof, which in turn fell in burying a section of No. 13 Platoon. Fortunately all the victims were speedily rescued, and although no one was killed, some were seriously injured. Just at this time the Rev. P. C. T. Crick, Senior Chaplain,

61st Division, was riding through the village, and joined the rescue party.

Despite the actual relief in being completely out of the line, life at Matigny for the Pioneers became very dull and uninteresting, and although the 61st Division was occupying the line, this was the only occasion in France when the 1/5th D.C.L.I. was not engaged on active duty.

ARRAS, JUNE AND JULY,
1917

Chapter III

Arras, June and July, 1917

The 61st Division's share in the Battles of Arras, 1917, was so minute that it leaves little to say about the doings of the Pioneers during that period. After the Battalion's stay at Matigny there followed an eight or nine days' trekking northward. On June 1st the 61st relieved the 37th Division, and the 1/5th D.C.L.I. took over the work of the 9th (Pioneers) North Staffs Regiment in the Arras sector.

At Arras the Battalion was split up somewhat. Its headquarters were in the Hotel de l'Universe, and the Companies occupied dug-outs in the forward area. The transport was at the entrance to the town on the Dainville road, where there were good billets for the men and fair horse standings.

Although the Arras offensive was dying down, the Germans were still very feverish, and despite the fact that no casualties to the Battalion resulted from shells in the town, the region near the station was badly knocked about almost each day. Aeroplane bombing was particularly active, especially near the transport lines, and on the evening of June 4th, during a lively raid, a driver was killed and two transport men wounded. In addition three horses were killed and nine wounded. The following night it was considered wise to move the horses away from the transport lines during 8 to 12 p.m.—the usual visiting hours of the bombing planes, but as Fate would have it, the horses returned synchronous with the arrival of the planes. Fortunately no damage was done although bombs dropped near.

The Companies in the line had a very unpleasant time during the Division's stay in this sector. The journeys each night to and from each respective task were indeed perilous, and casualties naturally occurred—both killed and wounded, 2nd Lieut. C. E. Vowles being amongst the wounded. The Battalion was, however, commended for its work by the C.R.E., 61st Division, who asked for the names of the Officers

(To face page 30)

ARRAS.

Drawn by E. C. MATTHEWS,
from a photograph by Major
T. A. KENDALL, M.C., 3rd D.C.L.I.

commanding companies during the tour in the line. The Company commanders were :—

" A " Company : Lieut. J. Trehane.
" B "   „   Lieut. H. R. Trelawny. *
" C "   „   Captain B. S. Hodge.
" D "   „   2nd Lieut. L. S. Leverton.

At the end of ten days at Berneville, to which the Battalion had moved after the shortest and most uncomfortable ten days it ever had in the line, it was reported that the Division had orders to move right back for a real rest. Consequently the Battalion packed up, and on the 21st journeyed to Le Ponchel, a little village a few miles from Auxi-le-Chateau. Whilst settling down in Le Ponchel, orders were received to proceed to Wavens, another small village only a few kilos away. And to Wavens the Battalion went, where a whole month was spent. Everyone thoroughly enjoyed this period of rest, and although a certain amount of training had to be completed, there was time for other diversions. The surrounding country was excellent for riding and fishing, and it happened to be on one of these excursions that 2nd Lieut. S. Hainsellin, a sporting combatant clergyman, left a fishing hook and bait lying on the ground. A hen, evidently

* Trelawny died in India on April 10th, 1921.

lacking powers of discrimination, grabbed the wriggling worm, hook and all, speedily devouring them. Needless to say, that feathered creature cost the sporting Priest more than a negligible amount, for hens were never cheap items on active service.

During this Divisional rest the Battalion took part in a combined programme of sports held at Willencourt, near Auxi-le-Chateau. A shield, offered for competition between the three Field Companies, Signal Company, Royal Engineers, and the Battalion's four Companies, was won by " B " Company, Duke of Cornwall's Light Infantry, which secured the highest number of points. The sports were so successful that it was decided to hold a dinner—the C.R.E. 61st Division, his Adjutant, Captain Fitzgerald, and also one of the R.E. Company Commanders, dined with the Battalion. The details of the evening are not particularly clear ! ! ! but one feature of the day's programme which must be noted was the holding of an inter-platoon competition, which comprised marching order turn-out, musketry, bombing, platoon drill, wiring, gas drill, and so on. The prizes were distributed by the C.O. on July 20th, when the Divisional Theatre Party " The Frolics " visited the unit and gave an open-air performance.

OFFICERS OF THE 1/5TH D.C.L.I.—JULY, 1917.

(Photograph taken overseas—Auxi-le-Chateau).

2-Lt. A. G. Hughes. 2-Lt. L. W Smith,
Capt. R. Coatsworth, R.A.M.C.
The Rev. J.P. Milum.
Lt. S. Hainsselin,

2-Lt. P. J. Morcom.
2-Lt. F. Soward.
Lt. H. R. Trelawny.

2-Lt. H. B. Trewella.
2-Lt. C. G. Dixon.
2-Lt. A. H. Paull.

2-Lt. W. Goldsworthy.
2-Lt. T. F. King.
Lt-Qm. Everett.
2-Lt. A. L. Poole.

2-Lt. W. H. Taylor.
Lt. W. Jeffery.
Capt. W. R. Potter.
2-Lt. T. W. R. Pengelly.

2-Lt. Piper.
2-Lt. W. Mould.
Lt-Col. T. Carus-Wilson.
2-Lt. L. S. Leverton.

2-Lt. W. L. Julyan.
2-Lt. A. T. Hunkin.
Major R. C. F. Fdyvean.
2-Lt. H. E. Ross.

2-Lt. A. McAllister.
Lt. J. M. F. Chomley.
Capt. F. Williams.
2-Lt. E. L. Coombe.

C. E. Vowles.
riner.
Hodson. Capt. B. S. Hodge.
lanchard.

All this was too good to last. The 1/5th
D.C.L.I. moved sorrowfully away from Wavens
towards Auxi-le-Chateau on July 26th, from
whence it eventually reached St. Omer, and from
there the march was continued to Noordpeene,
near Cassel. The rest of the 61st Division were
scattered about in the district awaiting instructions
to move into the battle area.

The month's training and re-equipping had
prepared the Pioneers for a next great chapter
in the Battalion's history—the Battles of Ypres,
1917, but had it been their choice . . .

THE BATTLES OF YPRES,
1917

CHAPTER IV

The Battles of Ypres, 1917

The 8th Corps (General Hunter-Weston's) was in reserve for the third Battle of Ypres, and the 61st Division was the only Division in the Corps. The commencement of the offensives was timed for July 31st by the 5th Army, which was conducting part of the operations with a portion of the 2nd Army.

At Noordpeene, the finishing touches were put on training and equipment, and all awaited instructions to move forward. The move was made on August 9th, and the Pioneers' Transport arrived at Vlamatinghe the same evening. The Battalion moved up in motor-buses, two Companies went straight on to occupy billets in Ypres, and the other two Companies, Battalion H.Q., and Transport occupied Warrington camp, slightly west of Vlamatinghe.

The first few days of the offensive had been successful to some extent, but the Germans

were obviously well prepared for our onslaught.
Pioneer work varied very much in the sector.
Wiring and consolidations were the principle
jobs, but cable trenches had to be dug, and
innumerable other tasks effected which the
situation demanded. And the work, whatever
its nature, was always attended with much
danger and many casualties. " C " Company,
the ' Railway Company,' was given a light
railway to construct near Goldfish Chateau, but
even that was unpalatable. There was hardly
a single point within a radius of five miles of
Ypres which could be termed ' safe.' ' Wipers '
was never a favoured part of the line, and particularly so during the Battles. At the time
of the third Battle, the Cloth Hall and Cathedral
were only framework. A point which could
not be reached by shell fire could be reached
by bombing 'planes, but invariably the same
place was subject to shelling by day and bombing
by night.

Of aeroplane raids there were several
particularly ugly ones on Warrington camp,
Vlamatinghe, and during one of these several
men were killed and wounded. Horses, too,
suffered very much, and in a very short time
promptly recognised the droning of approaching

(To face page 38)

"The Cloth Hall and Cathedral were only framework."

Drawn by Lieut. E. C.
Matthews, from a photograph
taken by him after the
Armistice.

'planes. Anti-aircraft guns were mounted at points here and there, but at that time little was known as to how Lewis guns should be used in case of raids. In fact, the Lewis gun was usually pointed in the direction from which the sound of the engine came. Occasionally, it is true, searchlights did manage to locate a 'plane, but in nearly all cases the time was too short for accurate sighting, and consequently firing was very erratic. This bombing took place nearly every night whilst Battalion H.Q. and the Transport occupied Warrington camp, Vlamatinghe. Although moonlight nights were thought to be responsible for most of the raids, there was practically no moon visible during August and September. But still they came.

It is difficult to give exact locations of Company billets and headquarters in the town of Ypres. As stated previously, " C " Company was at Goldfish Chateau, but " A," " B " and " D " Companies were in the town itself hidden away in countless cellars amongst the ruins.

There were two Battalion Headquarters— forward and rear. Forward was in the canal bank close to the Headquarters of the C.R.E., and rear was at Warrington camp at Vlamatinghe.

Pack ponies were used on three occasions for the difficult task of carrying forward pioneer material. The latter consisted of screwpickets, barbed wire, and such things. These ponies were loaded up at Ypres, and then led forward under direction of a Subaltern from one of the Companies in Ypres. The Officer detailed for this perilous duty had not only the task of leading the way to the place where the material was required, but controlling the convoy of mules or pack-ponies under shell-fire. This acute and double task seemed never to be fully appreciated by those who did not take part in it. The lonely, shell-striken roads at dead of night along the Ypres battle-grounds were nightmares—each road sharing the deadly fury of the enemy guns. To give orders to men during shelling is a trial but to try and control mules under similar conditions is well nigh impossible.

The Battalion casualties were amazingly light during this period. Not a single Officer was killed or wounded, and very few men, although every day some portion of the unit managed to get involved in a barrage or some shelling.

Towards the end of August, the Battalion was employed on work closely connected with the Passchendaele offensive, and frequently came under heavy shell fire. The scenes of labour are familiar to everyone who has followed the doings of the British Forces in France and Flanders in 1917. Steenbeck Ridge, Canal Bank, Pond Farm, St. Julien Road, Wieltje-Gravenstafel Ridge, Jew Hill, Oxford Road, rank amongst the places never to be forgotten. The Battalion remained in the Ypres salient until the middle of September, when the Division was withdrawn owing to heavy casualties to the Infantry Brigades. Later a move back was made to Reay—a camp a mile or so S.W. of Poperinghe, and here the Battalion stayed until a further move was made to former billets at Ochtenzeele, near Noordpeen

On the Division leaving the 5th Army, the following telegram was sent by the G.O.C., 5th Army, to the G.O.C., 61st Division :—

" With regret the Army Commander bids farewell to the 61st Division, and thanks all ranks for the good work they have done while with his Army. The Division has been a long while in the line, and successfully fought under trying conditions, and has largely contributed to wearing down enemy resistance on their front. He wishes the 61st Division all good fortune and fresh success in the future."

The G.O.C. 61st Division replied as follows :—

" Please express to the Army Commander my thanks for his heartening and inspiring message to the Officers and men of this Division. His appreciation of the work done whilst with the 5th Army has been conveyed to all ranks, and will brace the Division for further efforts."

The Battalion began its move from Ypres on Friday, 14th September, and on the 18th entrained at Esquelbec for Aubigny.

Arras once again was the destination.

BATTLE OF CAMBRAI.

1917

Chapter V

Battle of Cambrai, 1917

After Aubigny was reached the march was continued to Duisans, where billets were allotted. On September 21st, Corporal E. E. Fisher, of " D " Company, was presented with the ribbon of the Military Medal by the Commanding Officer on a Battalion Parade.

The stay at Duisans lasted until the 24th, on which day the whole Battalion and Transport moved towards the town of Arras.

Companies were again divided as regards billets. Battalion H.Q. occupied those excellent and popular dug-outs in the railway cutting near Athies. Two Companies also occupied dug-outs near by in the same cutting. The other two Companies went forward, and by a system of exchange billets introduced between Companies, all in turn shared the comforts of Athies.

The work of the Companies was of a forward nature. A new road was being constructed over the reserve line—presumably it was thought that the Germans were about to retire from this sector, and a new road was planned over the site of old trenches which had been captured in the spring of the same year. The road was made, but the retirement was not.

There was a good deal of trench work for the Pioneers—revetting and keeping existing trenches in repair. The front just at this time, September to October, 1917, was very quiet. Arras was rarely shelled. The Officers' Club flourished, and familiar figures would be seen flitting in and out, and everyone seemed quite happy, with the exception of those who had business near the chemical works at Fampoux.

But before the Battalion left Arras things livened up somewhat. On November 29th, Arras was shelled consistently, and the next day the Pioneers left Arras—(there is no connection between these two events). Orders had been received to proceed to a small village named Basastre, which was about eight kilos S.E. of Bapaume.

The Battalion moved by 'bus and the Transport by road. During the journey the destination was changed from Basastre to Ruyaucourt, and for the transport a continuous series of different

orders arrived every few kilos, but eventually
the Staff seemed content to allow this section
to go to Bertincourt, a village quite close to
Ruyaucourt, where it arrived after one of the
longest journeys it ever accomplished in France—
lasting from 7 a.m. until about 10 p.m. The
Battalion bivouaced in a field for the night,
and it was wondered by everyone why there was
so much change and uncertainty. Wild stories
were heard on all sides, and unfortunately true
ones too.

It appeared that the Germans were launching
surprise counter-attacks following the wonderful
British success of a week or so previous. The
latter commenced with the famous Tank attack
of 20th–21st November without any Artillery
barrage, which was followed up by the capture
of Bourlon Wood some days later.

The German attacks had come as much of a
surprise to us as ours had to them. We had made
immense captures in men and guns, and they
had done the same. It was thought that the
61st Division had arrived in the area for rest
and training, but owing to this sudden and
unexpected diversion on the part of the Germans,
the Division had to be used for checking any

further advance following the enemy's break-through.

The Battalion spent a very cold night, 30th Nov.—1st Dec., in the field near Ruyaucourt, but on the 2nd it proceeded to hutments on the Fins – Gouzeaucourt Road. From here the Pioneers went on working parties in order to construct a line on Beaucamp Ridge. Having completed this, a move was made to Havrincourt Wood, with rear Headquarters at Equancourt. Work was carried on in the front line, supports and reserves.

The Infantry Brigades of the 61st Division were severely handled during the next few days, and the 1/5th D.C.L.I. was busily engaged in constructing new trenches and consolidating. This was a trying time for the Battalion. Havrincourt Wood was subject to almost undivided attention of German guns and bombing 'planes.

Captain F. Williams, who had done excellent work with the Battalion, now left for the Tank Corps for duty as Workshop Officer, and 2nd Lieut. Dixon was wounded during tour of duty, and was evacuated to England.

The Transport meanwhile had moved to Equancourt, the sole residential building of which was a useful stable. The remainder of the village was in complete ruins. Nissen huts there were, but they were too far away from the horse lines to be occupied by the men, and although several visits to the village were made by enemy 'planes, there were no casualties to either men or horses.

On Christmas Eve, 1917, the Battalion said " Good-bye " to this area, for which no affection was nursed, moving to Etricourt, and from thence to Plateau Station via Bray-sur-Somme and Marly Camp, which was reached about midnight. The Transport had arrived a few minutes earlier, having travelled without loads owing to the extreme frozen state of the roads. The baggage and tools came by motor-lorry, also the Xmas Puddings.

Marly Camp, between the villages of Chuignes and Chuignolles, was not an ideal camp—especially in a foot of snow. The huts were of the French pattern, very big and high, and consequently extremely cold.

Christmas, 1916, was enjoyable, although the 61st Division was in the line ; but Christmas, 1917, was still more enjoyable. Looking back on this period, it calls to mind somewhat acutely that for a good number of Officers and men of the Battalion, that Christmas, 1917, was their last. 1918 was a sad year for the Pioneers, and a glorious one also, for then not only did they do their duty first as a Pioneer unit, but when the crisis came threw away the pick and shovel for the rifle, and faced the fierce onslaughts of the massed lines of grey which threatened the very gates of Paris.

The Battalion saw the end of the year fizzle out at Marly Camp; but immediately 1918 dawned, orders were received to proceed in the direction of St. Quentin.

BATTLE OF ST. QUENTIN,
1918

CHAPTER VI

Battle of St. Quentin, 1918

Marteville. The St. Quentin area was reached in January, 1918, and the greater portion of the Battalion (Bn. H.Q., " A," " C," and " D " Companies) occupied billets in Holnon Wood. " B " Company had billets in Marteville —a ruined village five kilos west of St. Quentin, which town was then just within the German lines. The horse lines were at Etreillers for some time, but were moved to Marteville on February 22nd. Billets as a whole were good, but the horse standings were particularly bad, as the ground almost approached a swamp.

Life was indeed pleasant for several weeks, as there was little shelling—only casual aeroplane raids reminded the trench dwellers that war still prevailed. Both sides were unusually quiet. The horse lines were well sheltered from aeroplane observation by trees, and numerous air photographs taken of the area by the R.A.F. failed to reveal anything conspicuous.

During February and the beginning of March, fears were entertained and many rumours were afloat over a coming German offensive in the sector. That this was thought probable in official quarters there is little doubt, for lines of trenches were constructed at various intervals as far back as Ham.

All four companies of the 1/5th D.C.L.I. were engaged on forward work, and it appears that only one casualty occurred—the Sergeant Bootmaker was badly damaged whilst converting shell cases into flower pots. But as time went on, and March 21st loomed nearer, excitement and keen expectation prevailed everywhere. Numerous ' silent ' batteries had been imported to the sector ; orders for a move towards Ham in case of a sudden German offensive had been issued. The Companies had definite Battle Positions allotted, and the Transport and Quartermaster's stores were to be moved on instructions to Lanchy—a ruined hamlet about six kilometres in rear.

There were three Officers at the Transport lines at the time—Lieut. A. H. Paull, Transport

Officer ; Lieut. A. L. Poole ; and 2nd Lieut. R. Chapple. As a rule there were always two Officers in charge of the Transport—a practice common to most Pioneer Battalions owing to the establishment of men and horses being about twice the size of an Infantry Transport. 2nd Lieut. Chapple had taken Lieut. Poole's place whilst the latter was on recent leave, and was remaining at the Transport in order to allow Lieut. Paull to proceed on leave—due to commence on the fateful morning of March 21st.

There was little to be done at the Transport beyond the usual routine of stable work, and the conveyance of rations to the various companies. R.E. material was sometimes carried for forward use.

The number of Officers at this time was increased far beyond the establishment of the Battalion. This resulted through the introduction of the new three Company organisation of a Pioneer Battalion, which effected the 1/5th D.C.L.I. on February 24th. But apart from this new arrangement, Officers continued to arrive from England, and some came from the 6th Battalion, D.C.L.I. That Battalion had been broken up on the formation of new Brigade establishments of three instead of four Battalions.

Contrary to G.R.O.'s two of the Officers at the Transport occupied their spare time by attempting to snare hares, but little success attended their efforts. During the evening of March 20th they set an elaborate ' hang ' outside St. Quentin Wood, and intended visiting it early next morning. Little did they dream of the dramatic events which happened to take the place of their proposed visit. The anxiety regarding the anticipated attack was at its height that evening, and rumour had ordered a German barrage at midnight which would continue until 4 a.m., at which hour the enemy would attack. This rumour was so persistent that many even made a few necessary arrangements in case of a hasty retreat. On receipt of " Man Battle Stations " from Battalion Headquarters, the Transport, as stated, would move to Lanchy, and there await further orders.

As Lieut. Paull was expecting to embark on leave early next morning, he went to bed, but the two other Officers decided to wait up until midnight to test the worth of rumour.

They waited, spending a very trying five minutes around midnight, listening intently for the first shell which would signal the attack. It did not arrive, and nothing happened excepting a few ringing barks from the British 6-inch guns close by.

At a quarter-to-one they both retired to bed thoroughly disgusted with rumour. One occupied a bed in the little mess-room, and the other two shared the same dug-out. Out of sheer bravado one of them slept in pyjamas.

March 21st. They had been sleeping only a short time when they were awakened by a most startling bombardment. There was a terrific din all round, and the earth shook violently with gun-fire and bursting shells. Every gun, on both sides, seemed to be firing, and was doing the deadly job with vengeance. There was a devil's own war going on between the British and German Artillery, and the three Officers were convinced that it was not a time for meditation. Consequently they were soon scrambling into their clothes—one trying to combine with this an endeavour to get into telephonic communication with Battalion H.Q. But the telephone, like most of its kind during times of emergency, failed to work. The wires had evidently been shattered by the heavy shelling.

They attempted to discuss the situation whilst dressing, but found that they had scarcely recovered sufficiently from the shock to hold a jointed conversation. Moreover, shells were constantly arriving which forced them to ' hold breath.'

Then Paull suddenly remembered his leave—and forthwith his vehement feelings towards the Germans were expressed in abundancy. There was little doubt that all leave would be cancelled.

Outside was absolute inferno—dawn had not yet relieved the landscape of its cloak, and the thick hanging fog combined with the intense enemy barrage tended to chill and bewilder. Overhead the shells were screaming ' whee-u, whee-u, whee-u ' in a mournful, melancholy strain. The prospect ahead looked black.

The Transport Officer despatched the telephone orderly to repair the broken line, then proceeded to the horse lines to see that things were in order, and whilst there issued instructions for completion of preparations for an immediate move. All the men had been carefully warned the previous night.

The signaller who had been sent out to repair the broken telephone wire, returned, and communication was again attempted with Battalion H.Q., but all to no avail. The line must have been broken in several places. The signaller, Private Penhale, also repaired the line belonging to a 6-inch Howitzer Battery close by. For this performance, and for other duties ably and fearlessly performed, Penhale received the Military Medal.

The Transport Officer on returning from the horse lines reported there were no casualties amongst the men, although several horses had suffered. One horse had been killed and several others severely wounded. A short time later a driver was wounded, and after being bandaged he was half led and half carried to the dressing station, which by this time was almost full.

There was little to do now until a runner arrived from Battalion H.Q. with orders. But could a runner possibly get through the barrage ? It seemed very doubtful.

Man Battle Stations. Still, a runner did arrive, looking more dead than alive, and handed over orders. This was at 6 a.m.— still quite dark.

Secret.

T. O.
1/5 D.C.L.I.

" MAN
        BATTLE
                STATIONS."

                A. G. HUGHES, Lt.,
Time   a/Adjt.,
5.30 a.m.   for O. C.
21/3/18.   1/5 D.C.L.I.

Immediately orders were given to harness up and hitch into wagons. All this was done with much trouble, as the horses were difficult to manage owing to the bursting shells. The Transport lines were unfortunately situated in a field adjoining the cross-roads in Marteville, and even in ordinary times cross-roads are not infrequently connected with horrors. But at break of day things became easier, and the Transport prepared to move.

It was arranged that one Officer should go ahead with the first wagon, and act as guide to the new lines at Lanchy—another Officer leaving the lines at the cross-roads last of all. There was no dignified exit as of yore. They departed in odd wagons and limbers at wide intervals, so as to minimise the effect of shelling on the highways.

Eventually the Transport assumed some kind of scattered procession, and turned its back for ever on the old lines at the cross-roads of Marteville. One Officer walked instead of riding, his horse having been killed a few minutes before, and the Transport Officer came last—riding in the mess cart, into which mess kit and gramophone had been hastily dumped. Some horses were wounded so badly that they had to be destroyed *en route*.

When the higher ground near Villevecque was reached, the fog became less dense, and the Transport reorganised into a presentable column. Between Villevecque and Beauvais the 2/4th Royal Berks were passed, led by Lieut.-Colonel Dimmer, V.C. In the rear of the Battalion the Colonel's groom was leading a horse. It since came to be known that this Battalion counter-attacked twice during that day, and Colonel Dimmer led the attack mounted on his horse on both occasions. Unfortunately in the second counter-attack he was killed.

There was little shelling along the roads further back, but there had been earlier on. The 2/4th Berks had 36 casualties at Ligny before they left for the line. The observation balloon at Villevecque had been completely demolished by a direct hit.

At 8 a.m. the Transport arrived at its new lines at Lanchy, and the billets consisted of the remains of a farm which had been destroyed by the Germans in their retirement of 1917.

The first duties were feeding of men and animals, and attention to wounds. The Veterinary Officer soon appeared and ordered the evacuation of several horses to the Mobile Vet. Section.

The Transport had now breathing time to consider what had happened, and moreover what was still happening. News from any reliable source was very scarce. However, it was quite clear that the Germans were making a stupendous effort on a wide front with the object of turning our flank at the point where we joined the French Army.

Holnon Wood. During the morning Lieut. Leverton and Lieut. Ross joined the Transport at Lanchy on their return from leave.

They had attempted to return to Holnon Wood, but were prevented by one of the Brigadiers at Attilly as they were not carrying box respirators.

HOLNON WOOD

DRAWN BY E.C.MATTHEWS, F.R.G.S.

SCALE 1:20,000

Wire ↗↗↗↗↗↗
Deep Dug-outs ☐

THE 1/5TH D.C.L.I. WAS HERE FROM THE MIDDLE OF JANUARY, TO THE TIME OF THE BRITISH RETIREMENT AT ST.QUENTIN, 1918, CONSTRUCTING NEW DEFENCE LINES IN THE BATTLE AREA. BATT. LEWIS GUNNERS HELPED THE INF.UNITS TO HOLD THE LINE.

NOTE: THE INFORMATION CONTAINED IN THIS MAP WAS GATHERED FROM FRENCH MAPS WHICH HAD NOT AT THE TIME, BEEN VERIFIED, MANY TRENCHES AND MUCH WIRE SHOWN HERE ONLY UNDER CONSTRUCTION.

Captain Potter who was with them was allowed to make the attempt on account of his position as Adjutant. Holnon Wood was being shelled by all manner of guns, and there was much gas in the air. The huts which were occupied by Battalion H.Q. and the Companies in Holnon Wood had to be deserted in early morning, and the excellent dug-outs in the cutting were utilised. The Battalion Orderly Room received a direct hit, also several of the surrounding Officers' quarters.

Lieut. H. R. Trelawny of " B " Company, with Lieut. Paull of the Transport, were due to commence leave together, and Trelawny braved the barrage between Marteville and Holnon Wood in order to obtain his leave warrant. On arrival he found just the remains of a Battalion H.Q., but worst of all, learned that all leave was cancelled.

Lieutenants Leverton and Ross seemed anxious to join their respective Companies, and as soon as box respirators had been procured, both started off to find their Companies. Leverton proceeded to Holnon Wood with Chapple who was taking up rations on pack ponies. Earlier in the day Major R. C. F. Edyvean, commanding the Battalion in the absence of Lieut.-Colonel Carus-Wilson on leave, had sent a runner asking for rations to be conveyed on pack ponies, as it was thought impossible for wagons to approach anywhere near Holnon Wood.

Chapple, who volunteered to go, began his perilous journey at 4 p.m., and attempted to establish the whereabouts of " B " Company— which was unknown. They had been billeted at Marteville it will be remembered. The cross-roads at Villevecque had received a direct hit from a shell which onwards prevented wagons passing this point owing to the crater formed. " B " Company, it was ascertained later, was in action near Massemy and the attempt at finding them at Marteville, was useless, and consequently failed.

During the whole day the fog lingered, even on the high ground, and as night crept on it became more intense.

Chapple's return with the pack ponies was awaited with anxiety, as it was then 7.30 p.m., but an hour or so later he did return. In his absence a German 'plane, even in the thick fog, had visited the Transport lines, but no bombs were dropped.

Chapple had a rather trying time. During the journey he had endeavoured to keep off shelled tracks, and therefore plunged across open country. A 5.9 had dropped near, causing a huge splinter to land on his steel helmet. This caused him some discomfort, but he still carried on his task of transporting the rations to the Battalion in a plucky manner. He was persuaded to see the Medical Officer about the wound, but he firmly refused, and some ten days later when the Doctor advised a few days' rest in Hospital, Chapple again refused to leave the Battalion.

He brought news of the day'e happenings. The H.Q. Officers and Officers of the two Companies in Holnon Wood had been forced to leave their huts, and to occupy the deep dug-outs in the railway cutting. The huts were mostly in ruins— a shell having passed through one hut, and incidentally had also passed through Lieut. Blacklock's bed a few seconds after he had vacated it. There had been a number of casualties in the Battalion during the day, both in killed and wounded, and although subject to heavy shell-fire the Pioneers had not yet taken part in actual fighting. Orders were expected at any moment to withdraw, and for a defensive position further back to be taken up.

News outside the battalion was very scarce. Nothing was known of " B " Company excepting that they were supposed to be engaged somewhere east of Marteville—having been attached to General White's Brigade, the 184th.

Just before midday on the 22nd March very cheering news came through, but very few really believed it. It was that the situation was " well in hand," and that the German Infantry had only reached our outpost lines. However, it cheered the men somewhat, and almost every day some bright ray of news reached the hard-pressed troops—even when we had retired twenty miles. Frequently accounts of great successes in the Ypres sector, at Arras, and so on, with extravagant numbers of prisoners, were passed on to the men, but it was never discovered who was responsible for their origin. There is no doubt that whoever the genius happened to be, he did an enormous amount of good for the time being. These exhilarating rumours rekindled spirits, acted as tonics, and it was not until the show was over that the troops learnt the actual truth.

At the Transport particular care was taken to have everything in readiness for a further move if sudden orders arrived. Near to the horse lines some men amused themselves with a football, whilst a Scotch Regiment were digging trenches in the same field.

A note arrived from Captain W. E. Potter, the Adjutant, stating that the Battalion (less " B " Company) were moving to Germaine—to which the rations were to be sent. Two wagons were also required, for bandsmen were discarding their instruments and acting as stretcher-bearers.

The Transport Officer left with the rations and wagons about two o'clock in the afternoon, and Lieut. Poole remained behind in charge of the rest of the Transport. Shortly afterwards men from various units passed by the Transport— some were obviously Brigade office clerks and Battalion orderly room clerks, as they carried bundles of papers and books.

Several were questioned about the situation, and one, a Brigade clerk, stated that the Germans had just entered Marteville as he left it. Shortly afterwards a battery of field guns took up a position close to the horse lines, and things began to look serious. As no orders arrived, Poole sent to the Brigade Transport Officer at Ligny, about a kilometre away, asking if any orders had arrived for a withdrawal. A Pioneer Battalion Transport was liable to be neglected when attached to a Brigade during a move. But the answer came back : " No orders yet, but you may move back as far as my lines if you wish to." A move was immediately carried out as far back as the Brigade lines, but on arrival there no orders were awaiting.

Although the Germans were comparatively near, there was little excitement at Brigade H.Q. Some individuals were certainly taking an interest in the proceedings, and one of the Brigade orderlies was seated astride a roof trying to view the battle through a telescope.

An hour passed and still no orders arrived. Eventually Paull returned with the ration wagon bringing with him instructions to move to a village called Canizy—a point about 3-4 kilometres W. of Ham. The Battalion was also proceeding there that evening from Germaine, excepting " B " Company, about which still nothing was known.

During the trek from Lanchy to Canizy, Matigny was passed at which the Battalion had been just ten months before. As the Transport passed through the village four German 'planes flew overhead, and the sensation of being sandwiched in a long column of transport stretching about a mile, with the prospect of a load of bombs being dropped from above, was indeed trying. Matigny still possessed an aerodrome, and in a short while several British 'planes were seen engaging the Germans. Within five minutes one German enemy 'plane was heading vertically towards gravity, leaving a trail of smoke behind. The other three escaped eastward. The 61st Divisional Headquarters were in the village, and the Divisional Commander watched the Transport march past.

Canizy. Canizy was reached about 5.30 p.m., and on nearing the village an Officer went ahead to secure billets and stables. He was met by several French women who eagerly asked for news. They seemed very anxious about Canizy.

There were excellent billets and stables in the village, and in one of the billets, a spacious barn, there were half-a-dozen Italian Labour Corps men who graciously offered to share their rations with the Transport men numbering 50. It so happened there was no necessity, as rations were always in abundance—thanks to the D.A.Q.M.G. 61st Division (Major Clowes, D.S.O.). A pleasant estaminet was found, and much omelette and "vin ordinaire" were eagerly absorbed.

Meanwhile we must return to events directly concerning the troops in the front line. Confirmatory news had come through from "Intelligence" that night—the Bosche were expected to attack the next morning.

The Platoon Commanders were nervous. True it was that wire existed between the enemy and the thin British line, but what is wire to the vengeance of a heavy Artillery, and the momentum of a vast attacking force ? It was also known that special defence trenches had been dug farther back, but would they prove effective and adequate ? Most of the men were almost raw recruits, hurriedly flung into the line to fill up gaps in the depleted ranks. Would they be able to withstand the fierce onslaughts of the morrow against which hardened troops might be prone to totter ?

These fears paraded themselves in the minds of the defenders, whilst the enemy away over on the other side were completing arrangements for battle under cover of the inky blackness. Terror lurked, and the mysterious night fog brought no comfort or relief to the anxious figures huddled along the fire-steps, O.P.'s and listening posts of the British line.

Suddenly a Very light shot up, and after culmination of height, gracefully returned to gravity with a melancholy thud. The Platoon

Officer on the fire-step took his chance during the illumination, and peered intently in front of him. A little on the left he detected a black object, and he gripped his revolver as firmly as the hand of an honoured friend. The shadow of the object cast a fantastical likeness to a human head and shoulders. Another Very light shot up, again from the same position, and the object which had attracted his attention had disappeared. The Platoon Officer gave a sigh of relief. Perhaps, after all, it was only an optical illusion.

Groping his way along the traverses and bays, he gave advice and encouragement to his men, at the same time trying to conceal his fear of the situation. Extra sentries had been posted, work suspended, and each man warned to use his eyes and ears to the utmost. When the time came they were to fight, if necessary, back to back.

The atmosphere itself that night seemed uncanny, and the silence of the usual artillery duel reminded him of the lull of an approaching storm at sea. He gazed at his watch. In a few hours daylight would be creeping over the dismal surroundings, and then, perhaps . . . perhaps . . . no one knew.

The men in the trenches were " standing to "—
their bayonets glittering in the obscure back-
ground of night. The Lewis Gunners were at
their posts of action, and the Platoon Commander was still nervously gripping the butt
of his revolver, when . . . the agony of suspense
was eclipsed by the clatter of a multitude of
guns, and the British Artillery, receiving the
S.O.S. call from the front line, responded with a
roar loud enough to awaken the dead.

To the Pioneers, the early morning of March
21st was not noteworthy for any particular
reason, except that it was more foggy than usual,
but about 4 a.m., however, those who were
employed in their usual work for the Division
were subjected to a violent shelling which caused
Battalion Headquarters to be moved into the
dug-outs at the railway cutting near Holnon Wood.
Half an hour later the order " Man Battle
Stations " came through, and " A " and " C "
Companies parade in battle order, and occupied
a line of redoubts, from which, however, they were
later ordered to withdraw.

" A " Company sustained several casualties
from shell-fire, and heavy shelling also forced
" B " Company to withdraw to shelters between
Marteville and Villeveque. Here they remained

until nightfall, and then " B " Company went into action with the 183rd Brigade. Meanwhile the Transport had moved back to Lanchy.

One among the many casualties on the morning of March 21st was that of the Bugle-Major of the Battalion. This gallant N.C.O., Bugle-Major Tucker, undertook the duties of Platoon Sergeant with " A " Company when ordered to Man Battle Stations. He was wounded, and whilst being carried to the Advanced Dressing Station a shell struck the stretcher and exploded, killing him outright. Tucker was a native of Bodmin, and a pre-war Territorial of old " E " Company.

In the early hours of March 22nd, Battalion Headquarters, with " A " and " C " Companies, occupied billets at Germaine, remaining there until noon, when they were ordered to dig positions N.E. of the village. Whilst so employed further orders were received, and the Battalion, leaving " B " Company still in action with the 183rd Brigade, proceeded across country to Canizy, to which the Transport had already moved earlier in the day.

ACTIONS AT THE SOMME
CROSSINGS

CHAPTER VII

Actions at the Somme Crossings

No sooner had the Transport settled down in Canizy than the Battalion, less " B " Company, arrived. The Officers and men were all very tired and hungry, as it had been impossible for them to have proper rest and meals since the morning of the 21st. This was a great reunion, and there was much to be told. It was feared that " B " Company had been lost, as it was said that they had last been seen at Marteville in Spooner's Redoubt, completely surrounded by Germans. This news was very distressing.

The estaminet supplied all the Battalion Officers' wants, and they fed in relays of eight at a time—partly because the room had a limited capacity for accommodation, and partly because sufficient food could only be prepared for eight at once. Practically all the Officers had lost their valises, and most of them " turned in " anywhere that night.

In one small room there were nine Officers—
one slept on the table, one underneath it, and
so on. The room eventually became an oven,
and very stuffy, which made sleep impossible
for a few.

During most of the night, a Naval gun, which
was very close to the village, maintained an almost
continuous fire, and did not omit to shake the
cottage every time it despatched its greetings
to the enemy. Aeroplanes were busy too—both
ours and the Bosche, there being a continual rattle
of machine-guns. These appeared to be just
above, but it was afterwards discovered that they
were on the ground, and fairly close by. One
Officer wandered outside to investigate matters
when the nearness of machine gun fire was dis-
cussed, and he returned with the alarming conclusion that enemy machine-guns were uncomfortably
near. The other Officers were aroused, whilst the
bitter facts were communicated to Major Edyvean.
Whilst the Major was receiving the news a Corps
Staff Officer arrived, and gave instructions for
the Battalion to form a line near the railway
just outside the village.

At 5 a.m. that morning, on March 23rd,
Headquarters with " A " and " C " Companies
again stood to arms, and took up positions

north of Canizy, where they dug in, and sent out patrols.

A further withdrawal was effected at 7 a.m. to positions along the railway cutting, east of the village of Hombleux, while " B " Company, which had so far only sustained a few casualties, proceeded to the transport under orders of the 183rd Brigade.

Verlaines. About noon " A " and " C " Companies were sent forward with orders to counter-attack and retake the village of Verlaines, which had previously been evacuated, and to hold the high ground north of the village.

These two Companies moved off in battle formation, with an advance guard, along the road towards Ham, and deployed for action on reaching a position about 4,000 yards from their objective. The band of the 7th Battalion D.C.L.I. played the Regimental March Past* as these companies deployed, and the moment was an inspiring one.

However, as the counter-attacking troops approached Verlaines the leading waves came

* Very little information can be ascertained of the origin of the Regimental March "One and All." It is stated to have been written by a lady residing near Bodmin, and to have been adopted by the Regiment early in the year 1811.

under heavy machine-gun and rifle fire from the enemy, who were in possession of the village, but pressing forward the Cornwalls drove the enemy out and gained their first objective by about 2.30 p.m.   Verlaines was ours !

The ridge to the north of the village was now under heavy Artillery fire, and very severe rifle and machine-gun fire, but the counter-attack swept on and carried the ridge.   The position was consolidated, but the Battalion suffered very heavy casualties during the process.

Captain Noel Tyacke, O.C. of " A " Company, had been instantly killed whilst leading his Company to the attack.   His second-in-command, Captain W. Jeffery, was seriously wounded in the head, and was not expected to recover.   A Subaltern of the same Company was also wounded.

The counter-attack of the village of Verlaines* near Canizy, although carried out with excellent results, will always convey sad memories to the Cornwalls.   The gallant band of Pioneers had

---

* A portion of the 2/4th Oxford and Bucks under Captain H. N. Davenport, M.C., also made a counter-attack against the town.   Davenport's men were " a disorganized mixture of many battalions, including, besides the Oxfords and other representatives of the 184th Brigade, a number of Cornwall's and King's Liverpools. They were unfed, and the demoralization of the retreat was beginning to do its work."   Davenport, the gallant officer, was shortly afterwards killed.

completely driven the Germans from the village, and pressed them back towards Ham, but . . . at a heavy cost. This brilliant action was carried out with such determination and success that the G.O.C. in C. deemed it fit to mention the Battalion in despatches which were published eight months later.

During the battle Captain W. E. Potter received a wound in the leg, but after having it dressed returned to duty immediately.

During the afternoon, evening and night, several enemy counter-attacks were made, but all were successfully beaten off and the position held. In addition, a flight of enemy aeroplanes caused many casualties by searching the position with machine-gun fire.

One of these in particular, flying very low, was the cause of much bitterness, but eventually this 'plane was successfully engaged by rifle and Lewis gun fire from the ground, and was seen to crash 300 yards in front of our position.

Throughout these operations the flanks of the Battalion were entirely open, both during its own attack and subsequent enemy counter-attacks.

On the following morning the enemy again attacked in force by both flanks and to the front.

Owing to the severe losses sustained, and in order to maintain an unbroken front as well as to conform to the movements of other troops, orders were given to withdraw. This movement was carried out in an orderly and methodical manner, although fighting was resumed the whole time. Heavy casualties were inflicted on the enemy.

Meanwhile the Transport was preparing to move to Herly, in the direction of Nesle. The Officers were soon busily arousing the men, and within a very short time the whole Transport left Canizy in the distance. It was approaching daylight when they rode away, and it was just possible to distinguish familiar forms in the semi-light. One remembers calling to several Officers, wishing them good luck . . . and to several it was the last time unfortunately.

As the bridge over the river at Voyens had been destroyed a few hours earlier, there was little danger of the drivers missing the Nesle road. One Officer went ahead with the first few wagons towards Nesle, while the other two brought along other portions of the transport. Near Voyens the Brigade Major of one of the Infantry Brigades of the Division was met, and asked for some news of the situation. He smiled, and said that he knew nothing, as he had been captured early the previous day, but had escaped from his escort, and rejoined his Brigade after passing through the German lines during the night.

As no definite orders had been received as to the Transport's destination, a halt was made outside Nesle, and the 61st Divisional Head-quarters approached for instructions. " G " Branch, 61st Division, was then at Rethonvillers, and was easily found. G.S.O.I. was greatly surprised when told that the Transport had been at Canizy all night, and it appeared that Canizy was actually at that time the front line area, and the Transport should have gone to Herly, about a kilometre west of Nesle. Orders had been issued for the Transport to proceed direct from Lanchy to Herly, but these had obviously gone astray.

However, things had turned out wonderfully well as it happened, considering the delicate situation, and an Officer rode back as quickly as possible to guide the Transport to Herly. Along the Ham–Nesle road there were crowds of refugees fleeing from Ham and the surrounding villages. They were all travelling westwards with as many household belongings as they could cram into their carts. Some, who were not fortunate enough to possess horse-drawn vehicles, carried what they could in wheelbarrows and even perambulators. A few were endeavouring to take away their farm stock — cows and calves, which proved very troublesome on the congested roads, as the animals repeatedly got mixed up with the Transport.

There were women, old and young, children and old men. All, who were able, carried a bundle of clothes or some household treasure. For a fair number, this was the second time they had been forced to abandon their homes. In 1914 they had been ruthlessly driven before the advancing enemy, but returned again in 1917, after the German retirement, to find in most cases their farms and cottages ruined. They had erected wooden huts amongst the devastation of their former homes, and after living in them for six or perhaps nine months, they were again compelled to leave them.

Their feelings towards the British did not contribute to a closer tie of the " *entente cordiale*," and very hasty but regrettable remarks were passed.

In Nesle itself everyone seemed anxious to get away as quickly as possible, as most of the inhabitants had already experienced the ordeal of German occupation of the town.

The Transport arrived at Herly about midday, and found an excellent space to park wagons. Good horse lines were found, but without cover. This was not of great importance, as the weather was gloriously fine during most of the retreat. Wagons were parked underneath some trees close to the remains of a chateau. It was not quite in ruins (through the German invasion of 1917), with the exception of several cellars underneath the outbuildings. Very soon the Transportmen were watering and feeding their horses, whilst a meal was being prepared for the detachment. They had only been in this place a very short time when to their astonishment and delight "B" Company marched into the Transport field.

They had not been captured—at least not all of them. It was delightful to have them back again, and everyone listened intently to all their grisly happenings during the preceding days. They described their glorious fight in Spooner's Redoubt from which they had escaped, although surrounded by Germans. The Officers declared that the men seemed to have entered eagerly into the fighting which had been hand-to-hand in several instances. But their casualty list was a sad one—mostly missing. By some astounding miracle not one of the Officers had been hit.

2nd Lieut. Beer of the Company had been detailed by the C.R.E. to blow up Marteville R.E. dump when the Germans captured the village, and this was carried out in a splendid manner at the very last moment when the Germans were actually entering the village.

" B " Company, during their fight in Spooner's Redoubt, managed to capture a German Major— a particularly fine specimen. And Lieutenant Ross, who always admired well-cut uniforms, could hardly refrain from asking the captured guest who happened to be his tailor.

After a good meal Officers and men stretched themselves out on the grass in the blazing sunshine, and after some doctoring of sore feet and application of boracic acid powder, they all slept very soundly. This was the first appreciable sleep they had had since 4 a.m. on the 21st.

The Transport made a few temporary improvements to their lines, but they were always on the ' *qui vive* ' for another hasty move.

Besides the Officers of " B " Company there were two other Officers with the Transport. These two Officers were in reserve in case of casualties, and were prepared to be called upon at any moment to proceed and join their respective Companies.

During the night German 'planes visited the neighbourhood and indulged in a couple of very spirited raids which, however, did no damage. 2nd Lieut. Coombe—better known as " Elsie " (on account of his initials E.L.C.), Lieut. Poole, and 2nd Lieut. J. Palmer slept in a very solid but extremely uncomfortable cellar, which possessed an easy-chair—obviously " scrounged " from Nesle.

" Elsie " occupied the chair, while Palmer and Poole slept on the floor—a cement one which did not greatly appeal to them. It was bitterly cold, and about midnight one of the Officers went on a stroll round the horse lines. Lieut A. G. Hughes, who was Assistant-Adjutant in the line, had returned to the Transport lines as a reserve Adjutant and he gave all the news of the day's battle. The remainder of the night at Herly was very quiet—there were no further bombing raids or anything otherwise disturbing.

The morning of March 24th passed without anything unusual happening, but the afternoon was full of incidents and excitement. From Herly one could see Nesle quite plainly. Near the railway station in the town, stores were being burnt to prevent them falling into the hands of the enemy, but as yet the Germans had not even commenced shelling the town—excepting a few ' heavies ' which fell around the outskirts.

At 3 o'clock floated a rumour—a startling rumour. Nesle was being occupied by Germans. The rumour was rapidly followed by a mounted Sergeant of the Division who galloped into the field and repeated the rumour. He also said that there was a general panic in the town— everything that could move was moving, and with the utmost speed. Motor lorries were travelling down the Nesle-Roye road three abreast—horses were galloping, and men running. All this sounded very alarming, and the climax was reached when orders were received from the Brigade Transport Officer to move at once in the direction of Roye. The Transport harnessed up in record time, and moved away—keeping an eye in the direction of Nesle. " B " Company accompanied the train, and intended acting as rear-guard in case of surprise.

There was a fairly hard track across country, leading from Herly into the Roye-Nesle road, and across this the Transport hastily wended its way.

When the head of the column reached the main road a halt was made—and to some this halt seemed unnecessary. Feverish thoughts of Uhlans flashed through their imaginations.

However, the halt had been ordered by one of the 61st Divisional Staff . . . AND THE GRAVE RUMOUR OF DEFEAT OF THE BRITISH ARMY HAD ORIGINATED IN NESLE BY A BOSCHE DRESSED UP AS A PADRE. The ball had been set rolling at first with unexemplified success—until it reached the 61st Divisional H.Q.

The Transport returned to Herly, and everyone felt better and more pleased with life than an hour before.

The Germans were still several kilometres away from Nesle, and as French reinforcements were rapidly arriving, there was no immediate cause for anxiety.

Some days later it was learned that the spy who had originated the rumour had been captured in Roye, but history does not relate what happened to him !

The night was comparatively peaceful—'planes arrived but did no damage.

March 25th was a fine day—almost rivalling the best day of the retirement. Between 9 and 10 o'clock the Colonel walked into the Transport field. He had just returned from leave, and seemed to be very pleased to be back again. Before he embarked on leave he had insisted on being recalled by the Division if the expected offensive developed. On this condition he went, and returned with all possible haste after receiving the message recalling him. He was delighted to learn of the brilliant counter-attack made by the Battalion on March 23rd. Very soon afterwards his servant had his valise unrolled, and producing his field clothes, the Colonel quickly changed from leave uniform. After a meal at midday the C.O. set out, taking " B " Company with him, in order to find the remains of the Battalion. Those who remained behind wished them all a cheery ' Bon voyage.' This was the last time they saw Carus-Wilson, ' Elsie,' or Palmer.

" Give my love to the Battalion." The farewell message of
Lieut.-Col. T. CARUS-WILSON, D.S.O.,
who died of wounds, 27/3/18.

The " block" of this photographic
illustration was kindly lent by Messrs.
Hiorns & Miller, Devonport.

" B " Company, led by the C.O.,
" Give my love moved forward into positions
to the along the Canal bank in front of
Battalion." Moyencourt, but further heavy
enemy attacks that day forced
" B " Company to withdraw, and it was during
this episode that Lieut.-Colonel T. Carus-Wilson
was mortally wounded while siteing battle
positions. As he was being taken down to the
Casualty Clearing Station he turned to his servant,
Private Stacey, and said, " Give my love to the
Battalion." He was placed in a hospital train,
but died before he reached Rouen. No Battalion
ever had a finer Commanding Officer, and of him
the men said, " If you want to find Carus-Wilson
you will find him in the line." His memory will
be cherished by the Battalion, above all for his
unselfish bravery, kindly disposition, and interest
in the welfare of his men. His own farewell
message, " Give my love to the Battalion," is
the best memorial of one who acted even as he
spake.

2nd Lieut. L. Coombe was also fatally wounded
on this date, and died at the dressing-station.

To attempt to describe the feelings of a
Battalion which had lost its beloved leader would
be invidious. Moreover, this volume will not

allow space for lengthy reflections, so we must resume our chronology. The Battalion, together with the Transport, after the loss of their C.O. moved from Herly. The Transport proceeded to Etalon, which place was rather less than a kilometre away. An Officer preceded the Transport and secured billets and horse lines at the village. The Mayor and his wife had just returned in a car in order to take away a few valuables which they had left behind when leaving the previous day. The Transport arrived, and everyone had excellent accommodation. The wagon lines were in a big farm-yard, and horses were stabled in the out-buildings, which, unlike many seen in France, were well built and extensive.

The Mayor (who owned the farm) had left behind some excellent cider, which had to be carefully guarded as the drivers were reported to be suffering from a perpetual thirst. A certain amount was allowed—but limited. Whilst unharnessing, several German 'planes intruded overhead, and some excitement ensued but no " eggs " dropped, as one driver described it.

Whilst they were, more or less, settling down, a despatch rider arrived with orders for an immediate move to Fresnoy-les-Roye, five or six kilometres away. This was the shortest stay they had anywhere during the whole retirement—just two hours.

There was some difficulty in moving, as the road seemed blocked with transport wagons and guns. The column extended quite a mile. During the halt G.S.O.I. arrived in his car, and endeavoured to discover the reason of delay. He pointed out that it was essential that they should move soon, but at the same time there was no cause for panic. As on this occasion, so during the whole of the retirement, the 61st Divisional Staff were continually encouraging the somewhat strained troops. And what troops would not feel highly-strung during almost overwhelming odds ? Utmost care had to be exercised and immediate steps taken to prevent any likelihood of disorder or panic. Nothing is greater or more important to a retreating force than cohesion, and history has recorded times without number how infectious panic is, and how rapidly it spreads. In a scientific war such as this, it was doubly indispensable that the morale of the troops should be maintained at all costs.

Eventually the obstruction, whatever it may have been, was removed, and the Pioneer D.C.L.I. Transport moved slowly forward—very slowly indeed, until a Battery of Field Artillery, which was in front, moved into an adjoining field where they took up positions for action.

Then the Transport moved more quickly.

Outside Fresnoy there was another long halt owing to the difficulty of finding room in the village for a whole Brigade of Transport, in addition to the Pioneer Battalion Transport. At last the latter were allotted horse lines and billets in an open field outside the village.

By this time it was quite dark, and the familiar buzz of aeroplanes could be heard in the distance. Everybody was immediately warned about lights —afterwards there was a period of listening and waiting. Presently several German 'planes flew overhead, deposited their loads some distance away, and disappeared. The D.C.L.I. were then given fresh lines in the village, and proceeded to occupy them.

Rations had been sent up to the Battalion before dark under instructions of the 184th Infantry Brigade, and in charge of one of their Officers. The rations had to be dumped at the 20th Divisional H.Q., to which Division the 61st was now attached, as far as " G " Branch was concerned. From 20th Division H.Q., the rations were sent forward by pack ponies from that Division.

After men and horses fed, and stable piquets were detailed, the day came to an end for most of the Officers.

March 26th, up to about midday, nothing remarkable took place, but shortly afterwards the rattle of machine-guns became very distinct, and anxious eyes were turned towards the road to see if the despatch rider with orders was in sight.

At length orders came, and the Transport moved away to Bouchoir, a small village which was just west of the old British line of 1917. One Officer, as usual, rode ahead to secure billets, and happened to pass over old trenches which the D.C.L.I. had occupied in March of 1917. It was interesting, but equally discouraging, to notice familiar trenches and dug-outs which " D " Company of the Pioneers had occupied the previous year. Was the war ever coming to an end ?

At Bouchoir excellent billets were obtained, as the Officer responsible for billeting knew the place well. About 4.30 the Transport arrived, and were comfortably settling down when they were presented with further orders to move.

This was to a village about six kilometres away—Fresnoy-en-Chaussee Marne. It had been designated a 'back area' at one time, and was never before visited by British troops.

Two Officers of the Transport, with grooms, rode towards the village. It was quite dark, and the moon had not yet risen. They happened to take the wrong turning, arriving at Hangest, but as it was only two kilometres from Fresnoy, little inconvenience was occasioned. On the way two Gunner Officers were found enjoying a meal beside a haystack, and after accepting some excellent red wine, the D.C.L.I. Officers continued their journey. The village of Fresnoy-en-Chaussee was quite unspoiled by war, and looked decidedly pretty as the mounted Officers rode down the main street. The moon had now made its appearance, and everything was very peaceful and quiet. Only a French woman, wearing a shawl and cloggs, betrayed that the place was not deserted. But as they passed down the street here and there a door would open cautiously, and one of the occupants of the house would take a searching look at the late intruders. Of one of these they enquired for the Maire, from whom some delightful billets were obtained without much difficulty.

The grooms were then sent to meet the Transport, and to conduct the ranks to their allotted quarters on arrival.

2nd Lieut. Hunt, who was back in reserve with the Transport, and engaged on this billeting expedition, persuaded the Mayor's family to prepare omelettes for the Officers who were in reserve with the Transport, and by the time they arrived an appetising meal was awaiting them. It was considered by the Officers that the Mayor and his family were the kindest people they had met in France—they did everything possible to make the short stay comfortable. After the meal the Officers slept on mattresses in the drawing-room of the Mayor's house—the first civilised quarters enjoyed in France for many months.

There was no necessity for an early rise on the morning of Wednesday, March 27th, so all the Officers, excepting the Transport Officer who saw ' stables,' lay on their comfortable mattresses and discoursed on the happenings of the past week. Each one felt convinced that no further retirement would be effected—at least it was thought that the old 1917 line would be defended.

At 8 o'clock the usual French breakfast was prepared—omelettes, roll and coffee. What British Tommy has not feasted like a Duke on omelettes and coffee in a village estaminet, and who has not expressed a liking for the long

French rolls of bread which Madam was usually seen carrying under her arm like an umbrella ?

About two hours later to the extreme delight of all someone shouted, "The Battalion is coming." It was "A" and "C" Companies— "B" Company followed about an half-an-hour later. The Mayor's women folk were again requested to cook and brew, and further admiration they earned.

The sequel was confusion. There were intense rejoicings, especially when "B" Company Officers met the Officers of "A" and "C," whom they had not seen for some time.

The marching and fighting had caused sore feet which had to be doctored and bathed. Fresh socks were provided by the few Officers who had managed to save their valises.

The re-union was great. Everyone talked furiously, and at the same time. But many familiar faces were not there—even the high spirits of re-union could not eclipse the thought of those who had fought their last battle. Many took to bed, as they were dead tired—it was their first real rest for days.

But this was too good to last.

The ' chug-chug ' of a motor cycle was heard outside.

A message for the C.O.

" The Battalion will move immediately to Mezières."

What again ?

The sleepers were aroused and the news conveyed to them. There were ugly sounds of bad language, and silence reigned whilst the Officers resignedly drew on their boots. Many were thinking hard as they did so.

Major R. C. F. Edyvean, who was now commanding the Battalion, detailed an Officer to ride to Mezières, the next village, and procure billets. In less than an hour the Officer was in the village, which was full of refugees and bristling village folk, who were hastily gathering together what they considered most valuable. They were preparing to evacuate. Some, however, were very obstinate, and merely sat by their fires and thought.

Three women folk who had ample room for billeting Officers and men refused to temporarily hand over one square inch of their home. It was tiresome trying to find room in this village, but at length accommodation was found for all.

The local gendarmerie served for H.Q., and a convent, which was also the local hospital, provided beds for all the Officers. While looking over the convent one of the nuns quietly questioned " Where were the Germans now ? " and " Were the British still retiring ? " Nevertheless, these nuns certainly seemed to be the least ' windy ' inhabitants in the place.

The Battalion appeared shortly afterwards with the Major riding at the head. He was wearing a borrowed pair of brown canvas shoes, as his feet were so swollen that ordinary boots were useless. After the location of billets was reported to him, guides conducted the Platoons.

Whilst this was being carried out a motor cyclist arrived and handed the C.O. two messages.

They were from Division. The Battalion was ordered to stand by after making a defensive line just East of the village. This newly received information was quickly passed round. Nobody was surprised—everyone was beyond caring. Discipline had a wonderful influence.

At 11.30 p.m., the Battalion moved forward to occupy billets at Le Quesnel, but on the evening of March 27th it marched to a point on the main Amiens Road, and embussed for Marcelcave, which they reached at 5.30 a.m. on March 28th. At noon the same day intense shelling of the village by the enemy made it necessary for the Battalion to evacuate the place, and to occupy trenches on high ground about one mile further south. This position eventually became the front line, and was held throughout March 29th in spite of heavy shelling.

The Counter-attack in front of Hangard Wood. On the morning of March 30th the enemy once more attacked, forcing back the Battalion on the right to such an extent that it was ordered to withdraw to a line running about 300 yards in front of Hangard Wood.

It was from this position that the Battalion, supported by the unit on its right, made a counter-attack which regained a portion of the high ground in front of them. But, the unit on the right having been held up, further advance was impossible, and eventually heavy machine-gun fire rendered the newly won position untenable, and the Battalion withdrew to their old line in front of Hangard Wood.

A second time the D.C.L.I. troops counter-attacked, but were held up by intense artillery and machine-gun fire, and were once again forced to .withdraw. They then consolidated posts in and around Hangard Wood. In spite of further heavy shelling they held on to these positions until midnight, March 30–31, when they were relieved by the Australians. They then marched back to Gentelles and occupied billets.

The same day saw them digging posts, etc., to the east of the village.

Meanwhile the Transport were ordered from Mezières to Jumel, which was about 12 kilometres away. A start was made about 4 p.m., accompanied by several Officers, who were to form a reserve in case of casualties.

The roads were filled with refugees' wagons and cattle. As the Transport neared Ailly-sur-Somme the moon was very bright, and in the direction of Amiens there were many flashes in the sky followed immediately by the ' thid, thud ' of dropping bombs. Amiens was being bombed.

After midnight the Transport was parked in the small square in Jumel, which appeared to be a small country town adjoining Ailly-sur-Somme, and so close that all seemed one town.

No billets could be found as the town was flooded out with refugees, so sleep had to be taken wherever possible. Two Officers slept in the mess-cart, and spent a very cold night in awkward positions. Mess-carts were certainly not adapted for sleeping quarters.

The next morning they were more fortunate, and secured quite a comfortable villa for Officers' quarters. A piano on which Lieut. Morcom performed, lent pleasure for the time. But during the afternoon the inevitable despatch rider arrived once more. He had appeared with distressing regularity since March 21st.

This time they were to go to Hailles—a tiny village situated a few miles south of Gentelle and Villers Brettoneux. This was not retiring, but side-stepping.

Later on they discovered that the Battalion had been conveyed by 'bus from Mezières to Marcelcave, and went into action east of that village.

Hailles was still inhabited when the Transport arrived, although the villagers expected orders to evacuate at any moment. There were plenty of eggs to be obtained, and the Officers' menu at all times included, and sometimes wholly comprised eggs. The menu sounds uninteresting, but an expert chef was available, and he was clever in that he could produce eggs in so many different forms. Constitutionally each course was the same, and yet graphically different.

During the night a drum was loudly beaten in the village street by an old man—probably a town crier of some sort. He was shouting "Evacué," and all the inhabitants immediately "evacuéd"—to goodness knows where.

The next day a visit to the Mairie was made, including an inspection of helmets of the village firemen. Several were tried on by the Officers, but were considered non-effective for active service.

Lieut. H. R. Trelawny and Lieut. T. W. R. Pengelly appeared during the morning, having been sent back to rest. Two Officers in reserve then proceeded to Marcelcave to replace them.

Lieut. Chapple took the rations up to Marcelcave, and had a very lively time. He only escaped being a probable casualty by hanging on to a field-cooker which was being drawn by a horse galloping out of the village. The shelling was very severe.

On Easter Sunday, March 31st, the Transport moved from Hailles to Le Paraclet, near Cotenchy. While the Transport moved to this place Lieut.

Poole took rations up to Villers Brettoneux, and tried to find the remains of the Battalion which were supposed to be somewhere in the neighbourhood. Arriving at Villers Brettoneux during a little " straffe " he found the streets almost deserted, except for a few " scroungers." Amongst these he discovered two men of his old Platoon. One was carrying an old sack on his back filled with evil-smelling fish. Poole enquired where he could find the Battalion, and where the rations could be deposited.

He was told that the remains of the three Companies were mid-way between Villers Brettoneux and Marcelcave, and also that it was quite possible to get there in daylight.

All this he believed, and started.

About 300 yards east of Villers Brettoneux he found the Battalion, and dumped the rations close by.

Just as unloading was completed Fritz decided that they were taking too long over the operation, and ventured to hasten them by sending over a ' pip squeak.' Expecting further tributes, Poole and the wagons dashed away, and in a few seconds could not be seen for dust.

He took the wagons back to Le Paraclet, and found the Transport in this tiny place mixed up with various Regiments and Corps—rear Brigade (184) H.Q., R.A.M.C., A.S.C., of a Cavalry Division, and so on.

The village possessed an enormous building—a School of Agriculture, which was turned into an excellent billet.

There were no civilians in the place—they had fled long before, but they had left behind several pigs which, of course, were not seen walking about for long.

At 8 p.m. on April 1st, two Officers started out— this time with cookers in full blast. The remains of the 1/5th D.C.L.I. were coming out of the line, and the Officers were to meet them at Gentelle. They were also responsible for finding billets there, and feeding the troops when they appeared.

In the cookers was stew, steaming hot, and in the stew were several fowls—place of origin unknown. Also secreted in one of the secret chambers of a cooker were several bottles of wine— again place of origin unknown.

They had, like the fowls, simply arrived.

Gentelle was in a shocking state—not from Bosche shelling, but several British Divisions had passed through during the last few days, and consequently, as the village had been evacuated and owing to lack of time, the interiors of houses were not as tidy as they might have been.

The two Officers found quite a good cottage for an Officers' Mess and billet, and they both commenced putting things in order, after having detailed a man as ' look-out ' for the Battalion.

They soon completed preparations for the unit's arrival, and waited until long after midnight, when they decided to sleep in turns. One kept the first and only watch, for the other could not have been asleep long before the Battalion arrived.

After having food, the Battalion fell into a well-earned slumber.

The next day Lieut. F. Soward went back to Bontillerie. This Officer, two days before when senior Subaltern in the line, had accomplished the wonderful feat of leading six counter-attacks in one day, across the open country between Villers Brettoneux and Marcelcave.

The remains of the Battalion had to stay at Gentelle until relieved two days later, April 5th, and during this time reorganisation was carried out. Captain Blanchard was the senior Officer, and consequently assumed command, and 2nd Lieut. C. E. C. Hughes, Acting-Adjutant.

The 61st Division then left the Villers Brettoneux sector, and the 1/5th D.C.L.I. moved back to Tailly by 'bus—right out of the fighting area. The Transport in the meantime moved to Cagny.

The Germans were now well held in this sector, but as a fighting force the Division was quite worn out. Rest and reinforcements were the only things which could bring them back as a fighting unit.

Thus ended, for the time being, their share in the heavy fighting. The great first stage of the German offensive was over, and the British retirement from St. Quentin was slowing down, and as far as the 1/5th D.C.L.I. was concerned was an event of the past.

The Battalion had abandoned picks and shovels, and had taken its place alongside the Infantry, and, moreover, had fought the whole way from St. Quentin to Villers Brettoneux at a terrible cost of :—

The casualties during the retirement from St. Quentin were :—

(To face page 103)

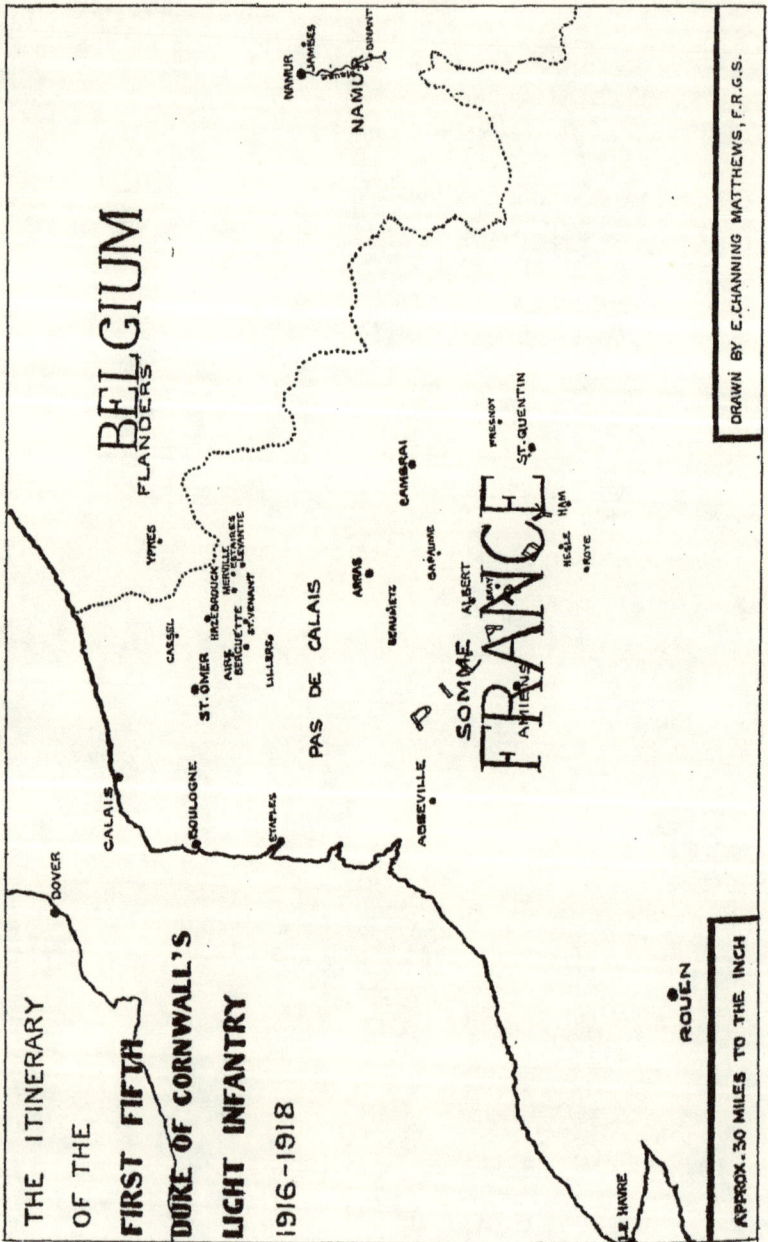

THE ITINERARY OF THE FIRST FIFTH DUKE OF CORNWALL'S LIGHT INFANTRY 1916-1918

DRAWN BY E. CHANNING MATTHEWS, F.R.G.S.

APPROX. 30 MILES TO THE INCH

OFFICERS.

Killed.

Lt.-Col. T. Carus-Wilson.
Capt. C. N. W. Tyacke.
Lieut. H. J. Palmer.
2nd Lieut. L. C. Beer.
2nd Lieut. L. C. Coombe.

Wounded.

Capt. W. E. Potter (Adjt.).
Lieut. A. G. Hughes (Asst. Adjt.).
Capt. W. Jeffery.
Lieut. L. S. Leverton.
Lieut. J. F. Chomley.
Lieut. H. C. Lorimer.
Lieut. W. Taylor.

Sick.

Major R. C. F. Edyvean.
2nd Lieut. P. Jane.

Evacuated.

2nd Lieut. Luscombe.
2nd Lieut. Stanlick.

Also wounded but not officially reported.

Capt. F. J. Blanchard.
2nd Lieut. R. C. Chapple.

MEN.

Killed	...	...	30
Wounded	...	...	139
Missing ...	...	...	30

MERVILLE AND FORÊT DE NIEPPE

CHAPTER VIII

Merville, and the Forêt de Nieppe

On April 5th the Battalion moved away from the fighting area to Taleu, and there occupied billets. During the next few days there was a rapid change of Commanding Officers.

Captain F. J. Blanchard was acting C.O. during the latter part of the retirement from St. Quentin, and for the first day afterwards. Captain E. M. Hodson reported back from leave on April 6th (the day following the arrival of the Battalion at Taleu) and took over command from Blanchard. Then Captain B. S. Hodge appeared, and took the reins for nearly a whole day, until Major R. C. F. Edyvean returned from hospital. Edyvean was just settling down when Major E. B. Ward, 2nd Battalion, D.C.L.I., arrived, and took permanent command of the Battalion. Five Commanding Officers in a few days might indeed be a singular record.

During Captain Hodge's short and temporary command, Major Christie-Miller, of the Bucks Battalion (O.B.L.I.), brought a draft of over 400 O.R. from the 4th (Reserve) Battalion

D.C.L.I. Most of these were under nineteen years of age, and all were entirely untrained for forward active service conditions.

The experience of bringing these youngsters up to the line was so extraordinary that it warrants a fairly full description. It was all the more extraordinary because the draft, although troublesome then, did so well later in the actions of Merville and the Foret de Nieppe.

The draft was handed over to Major Christie-Miller by the Authorities of H. Infantry Base Depot, and entrained at Etaples. A nominal roll and all papers completed the arrangements, but it became clear when the Major saw them being entrained that his hands would be pretty full.

They all left Etaples in the middle of the morning of April 5th, and after leaving Abbeville the destination was given as Saleux, a few miles south-west of Amiens. But enquiries *en route* disclosed that this was 'rail-head' for Divisional H.Q. and the Artillery only, and that the Infantry were at the other end of the area. So the party were to be detrained at Ailly sur Somme, which was reached about 5 p.m. It then transpired that they should have been detrained at Picquigny, which was 4—5 miles nearer the D.C.L.I. unit.

The journey had been uneventful, except for such dangers as arose for individuals who spent the time climbing on the top of the carriages.

To assist the Major there was one Company Sergeant-Major and one Company Quarter-Master Sergeant from the Base Depot, but no other Officer or N.C.O.

On arrival at Ailly, some two hours were spent in trying to arrange for a train back to Picquigny. When that failed an endeavour was made for motor lorries from Division to take the party to the 1/5th D.C.L.I., a distance of 12 miles.

From what the Major had seen of the draft, he did not relish the task of marching them that distance, starting at sunset. The next thing to be done was to billet them—no easy matter in a village allotted to another formation and then stacked with troops.

Eventually the Town Major gave accommodation for 100 men, and put Major Christie-Miller in touch with a Labour Company believed to be in possession of some tents. These people treated the Major with the utmost consideration, and the remainder of the draft were stuffed in tents—21 per tent, after these had with difficulty been pitched.

This took until 10 p.m., and in the meantime the C.Q.M.S. was trying to get the men some tea.

It is not everyone who realizes how helpless men are away from their units, and in this case without any cooking pots or fuel. The men did not know how to cook in mess tins—even if some fuel had been looted. Eventually an adjoining Infantry unit boiled up their cookers, and the draft provided with tea by midnight.

The camp became a pandemonium when the Major tried to get the boys to bed, as they had retold off the tent parties, and the unpopular men were left outside to manage somehow for themselves.

The Major found a place on the floor of the school, but did not get much sleep.

The youngsters were awakened at 6 a.m., and were ready to move off by 7 a.m., after feeding them through the same Infantry Battalion.

By this time it had become obvious that they were totally devoid of discipline or training, and it began to be whispered that they were unfit as well, *i.e.*, "B.I." So in the absence of N.C.O.'s (except the two from the Infantry Base Depot), the Major began to have misgivings about the march of 12 miles with full kit, ammunition, and blankets without the discipline which would hold troops together under such trying circumstances.

The start of the march revealed the troubles there were to be. The boys were divided into 10 platoons of 40, with an interval of 10—20 paces between platoons. The C.S.M. was put in front with a map, and the C.Q.M.S. and the Major marched in rear to "whip in." The platoons were nominally under the command of "provisional" Lance-Corporals, but actually were commanded by a small committee consisting of the most insubordinate. Before they had marched half-an-hour, 20 had fallen out, and most of them explained the nature of their ailments which caused them to be marked "B.1." And moreover, the regulations in England which provided against such troops being marched more than 5 miles.

The 20 "crocks" were put into a party in rear, and allowed to lose a little distance, which was made up at the halts, and many were subsequently sent back to their platoons.

The "falling out" became fast and furious, and quite early in the march had reached 40. These were put in rear, and coaxed along with soft words and lashed with the tongue according to the temperament displayed.

On one of the first hills within 4 miles of the start, the whole column fell out on both sides of the road, and eventually the last platoon which was driven from behind appeared near the head of the column which had by this time become inverted.

Matters would have gone badly but for the assistance of a " Graves Registration " Officer who seeing the difficulties left his work for a few minutes to help. He started at one end of the column, and the Major at the other, and they reformed the Platoons for another start.

Subsequently the draft started a new device when a hill was reached. They passed the word forward to the C.S.M. in front as a message from the Major that the column was to halt. On one occasion they played this within 10 minutes of the commencement of a marching period.

About 5 miles from the start, the road went down into a valley, and came up the other side in the form of a hair-pin. The Major's feelings can be imagined when his warriors broke ranks in tens and twelves and went across country to the opposite hill.

It was soon after this that the situation was saved by a mounted Officer, and two mounted N.C.O.'s sent by the Battalion to meet the draft. Two motor lorries also appeared on which they were able to load the blankets and some of the great coats, and also one or two men who could be got no further.

With the mounted Officer and N.C.O.'s distributed down the column, the discipline improved. The attempts to halt on every hill were frustrated, and ring leaders had their names taken. The state of discipline can be best illustrated by the fact that the mounted Officer was loudly "booed" by two platoons in the centre of the column for preventing these irregular halts.

The march was duly completed and the distance of 12 miles covered in 8 hours with no (ordered) halts beyond the regular clock hour ones, and one for discarding blankets. This will give some idea of the difficulties which had to be encountered.

The only way to get these boys or youths in was to see that everyone was kept in front. It was no mean achievement that all finished the march on their feet except six, of whom four were left unconscious and two had sprained ankles. These were brought in by lorries and an ambulance.

This draft consisted entirely of boys under 19 years, and were to form the backbone of a Battalion which had suffered heavily in the retreat.

Within 7 days the Battalion was flung into the Lys Battle, east of Merville, and for two days bore the brunt of the fighting until the battered remains were relieved and extricated by the arrival of the Infantry of the Division round St. Floris on April 12th and 13th.

After handing over this draft to the Battalion which was billeted in the adjoining villages of Laleu and Metigny, Major Christie-Miller went on in the blanket lorry to report to Divisional H.Q. located in a charming chateau at Pissy.

Major E. B. Ward then commenced the reorganisation and re-equipping of the Battalion, and Captain E. M. Hodson was appointed Adjutant. Company Commanders had a busy time, during which information was collected in respect of casualties incurred in the recent battle.

Before any organised Battalion training could be undertaken, orders were received for all to hold themselves in readiness to proceed to the Merville sector—and many had hopes of a well-earned rest. Lieut. H. E. Thompson, R.A.M.C., then arrived to replace Captain R. C. Coatsworth, R.A.M.C., who was in Hospital.

At 10 a.m. on April 10th the Battalion and Transport, less " C " Company, marched to Hangest-sur-Somme and entrained. The detraining station was Steenbecque, and the journey there was quite uneventful—cold and cheerless, like most other " hommes 40 chevaux 8 " journeys on the B.E.F. Service. An aeroplane accompanied the train—a defensive action against probable hostile bombing 'planes. It was the first time that the 1/5th D.C.L.I. troops had been honoured and protected during their moves by the Royal Air Force.

On arrival at Steenbecque darkness was beginning to creep over the landscape, and the Battalion was met by several Staff Officers of the 61st Division, who imparted alarming information.

The Germans had made an attack between Fleur-baix and Givenchy at the time the 61st Division was in the midst of entrainment from Amiens. In front of Levantie the Portuguese received part of the blow, and retired. These proceedings resulted in the flanks of neighbouring British Divisions—one of which was the 51st, being exposed.

" A " and " B " Companies of the Cornwalls occupied billets at Thiennes, but at 2 a.m. on April 11th these two Companies were sent forward to join the 153rd Brigade, 51st Division, as they were some of the first troops to arrive, and therefore nearest to hand. Owing to breakdowns and congested traffic, trains were very late in arriving at detraining stations, and units detrained at intervals covering a period of 48 hours, commencing on April 10th.

The XIth Corps Cyclist Battalion arrived soon after the German attack commenced, leaving their bicycles on dismounting. They promptly went into action with the object of checking the advance. But the arrival of this Battalion was apparently misunderstood by our gallant Allies, who regarded the bicycles as a "gift of the Gods" and rode away.

No definite orders were given in respect of the 1/5th D.C.L.I.'s share in this battle until 2 a.m. the next morning at Thiennes, as stated. The Battalion had marched to Thiennes after detraining the previous night. Orders then came through for the Battalion to take up a line east of Merville in place of the scattered Portuguese, and attempt to check the German advance.

It would be difficult to describe the actions or follow the movements of the various units concerned, but mention must be made of the very gallant fight put up by the 1/5th D.C.L.I. for over 48 hours prior to the arrival of sufficient troops of the Division with which to establish an organised line.

The fighting strength of the Battalion at this time was 24 Officers and 944 other ranks, consisting largely of drafts received during the previous four days. The whole of the drafts consisted of youngsters, without any experience of real warfare, and this sudden plunge from the barrack-square to the firing line, and, moreover, into a really stiff fight against a well-trained enemy, was indeed a terrible calamity. Still, there was nothing but praise for the manner in which these youngsters conducted themselves, and officers and men who had been out in France continuously for two years or more, spoke very highly of these young soldiers, who played their part so nobly in holding up the advance and defeating the enemy in his objective—the capture of the Channel ports.

The official summary of the 61st Division states : " The D.C.L.I. had debussed at Calonne, and had commenced to dig in on a line from the fork roads at Bouzateaux Farm to Meurillon. The work of organising the line was rendered extremely difficult owing to intense machine-gun fire from Paradis, L'Epinette, and the copses west of Lestrem. These two Battalions (2/6th Royal Warwicks and 1/5th D.C.L.I.) were now holding a front of over 5,000 yards. Throughout this period a constant stream of traffic—Infantry, R.F.A. and Portuguese, passed through the front lines. The Portuguese could not be checked, but about 100 stragglers of the 51st Division were collected and put into a defensive position on the right flank to fill a gap north of Vertbois Farm, though the men were incapable of further fighting without food and rest.

The Divisional summary of the fighting. At 6 p.m. this line from Bouzateaux Farm northwards to the Lys Canal was strongly attacked, and the left flank of the 1/5th Duke of Cornwall's Light Infantry was turned; there being at this time no touch with any troops south of the canal. The timely arrival of the 3rd Company (" C " Coy.), together with the elements of the 5th Gordon Highlanders, enabled the line to be reformed, with its left flank resting on the river Ancienne-Lys, immediately west of Grand Pacout. This line was maintained throughout the night. Early on the morning of April 12th a general attack developed along the whole front, and by 5.30 a.m. the enemy had worked round the Duke of Cornwall's Light Infantry right flank at Vertbois Farm, and had penetrated the line at several points, entering Pacout and taking our troops in enfilade with his machine-guns.

A stand was made by the 1/5th Duke of Cornwall's Light Infantry in front of Calonne, with the aid of some elements of the 51st Division, but their right flank soon came under severe machine-gun fire from the direction of L'Etang Farm. Considerable casualties were inflicted on the enemy, who showed great boldness in pushing forward his machine-gun detachments. Successive stands were made along the railway S.E. of La Hennerie, and on the bank of the Lys Canal south of Sarc, but the enemy had by this time come through Calonne in considerable numbers, and, working forward, had got through the junction of the forward companies of the 5th Gordons and the 9th Royal Scots, leaving no alternative but for the Gordons and the 1/5th Duke of Cornwall's Light Infantry to withdraw across the canal. This crossing was effected at noon, under heavy and accurate machine-gun fire from the north bank of the Lys in the direction of Merville. The casualties to the 1/5th Duke of Cornwall's Light Infantry in this action were 16 Officers and 467 other ranks."

Meanwhile the Officers and men at Transport away back a few kilos were anxiously awaiting news. Those who were 2nd-in-command of Companies had been left out of the fighting as a reserve when the Battalion left Thiennes. No definite information arrived, excepting through some refugees from Laventie, to whom some of the Officers were known. But they could impart no connected account of the fighting, nor append anything to happenings, excepting only as far as they were immediately concerned.

An Officer started out with the ration wagons during the afternoon with the object of finding the Battalion. He approached Calonne-sur-la-Lys, but found himself in the midst of a number of Cornishmen and Scotchmen who were engaged in a hot fight against some Germans. He helped to rally numbers of men who were thoroughly demoralised owing to the hard fighting during the day.

On his return he brought a tangible account of the day's happenings—there was a deplorable roll of casualties and a chaotic mix up of Regiments and Divisions.

During the early part of the afternoon of the following day, 2nd Lieut. Robson returned to the transport lines with 11 other ranks, and seemed

quite confident that this small party was all
that remained of the 1/5th D.C.L.I. He had
been given orders to return to the transport
lines by a Colonel of the Division. No concrete
information was extracted from him—everything
still appeared to be in disorder.

Shortly afterwards instructions were received
to send up rations to 61st Divisional H.Q.,
"G" Branch, at a certain map reference,
and an Officer started out with a couple
of limbers containing the rations whilst it was
still daylight. The roads in this area were
particularly difficult to follow, even through
the aid of a map, and it was quite dark before
61st Div. H.Q. "G" was reached. On the
journey a French gentleman was encountered
who had recently been liberated from the lunatic
asylum at St. Venant, and this individual unfortunately had not been of considerable use
in helping to find the map reference.

At "G" Branch, 61st Division, everyone
seemed to be extremely busy, and all had the
impression that the situation was well in hand—

in fact, one General Staff Officer had both his hands tightly bandaged.

Information was received from G.S.O.3. that the remains of the Battalion were being withdrawn from the fight, and were to be met outside St. Venant at " P " 9.6.7.10. (Sheet 36a : 1-40000).

On the way to this map reference from Divisional H.Q. the Officer observed with alarm that a German 'plane was taking an unusual interest in the road. A marked curiosity was also exhibited by the airman towards a dump-fire at the station of St. Venant, but no bombs were dropped.

A good cottage was found to provide an Officers' billet, and barns were allotted for the men—numbers could only be vaguely guessed.

While engaged in this search for billets, Captain Trehane, Lieut. Johnson and 2nd Lieut. Edwards appeared with a large party of men—the number in which it was impossible to estimate in the darkness. They, like Robson and his party, claimed to be the sole survivors of the Battalion, but, fortunately, they were not even the sole survivors of a Company. Around the billets there was a very distinct smell of gas following some shelling which had taken place a few minutes previous, and Captain Trehane was compelled later to move all the men owing to continued gas shelling.

During the following day, April 13th, the remainder of the Battalion joined Trehane's men outside St. Venant, and the appearance of the C.O., and Lieut. F. Soward, caused much surprise, as they had both been seen quite dead the day before! After the usual washing and cleaning, a thorough reorganisation was necessary. Capain Trehane was appointed Acting Adjutant; Lieut. E. C. Davies, O.C. " A " Company ; Lieut. T. W. R. Pengelly, O.C. " B " Company; and Lieut. J. C. Johnson, O.C. " C " Company.

Severe Casualties. The casualties during the past few days had been very severe—16 Officers and 467 other ranks, killed, wounded and missing.

L

The Officers casualties were as follows :—

Killed.

"A" Coy. Lieut. T. Goldsworthy,
Lieut, L. W. Smith, and
Lieut. P. J. Morcom.

"B" Coy. None.

"C" Coy. 2nd Lieut. R. Chapple.

Wounded.

"A" Coy. 2nd Lieut. Aedy.

"B" Coy. Captain E. M. Hodson,
Lieut. H. R. Trelawny,
Lieut. G. G. O'Carrell,
2nd Lieut. C. E. C. Hughes,
2nd Lieut. Green,
2nd Lieut. W. F. Smith,
2nd Lieut. W. G. Hunt, and
2nd Lieut. Drewitt.

"C" Coy. Captain B. S. Hodge.

Missing.

"A" Coy. 2nd Lieut. H. Blacklock.

"B" and "C" Coys. None.

By this time, April 4th, the whole of the 61st Division was in the line, and the Battalion resumed pioneering once again. Battle positions were allotted to the 1/5th D.C.L.I. which ran from about 1,000 yards E. of St. Venant northward towards the Haversoerque–Merville road. This line was to be held by the Battalion in case of further enemy attacks, but fortunately the manning of battle positions never took place, and all three companies carried on with their respective jobs.

St. Venant. Some of the billets near St. Venant soon became untenable owing to frequent shell-fire, and new quarters had to be found further away from the town. A few hundred yards in rear were several good farms, and to these " B " and " C " Companies migrated. " A " Company remained in billets just outside the town. The Battalion had quite a respectable cottage for Headquarters, and seemed quite happy until an enormous shell arrived, which left a crater of monstrous description. For a time the feeling of security was dispelled, and it was decided that H.Q. had narrowly escaped total demolition by a ' short ' for the Isberges Steel Works.

The move of the Battalion, and " B " and " C " Companies, was carried out on May 4th. Previous to this 2nd Lieut. W. F. Smith was wounded by a shell splinter.

Each week a party of the latest joined draft was sent to rear Headquarters at La-Roupee, and given a week's training in drill and musketry. This week was also intended to serve as a week's rest—but no allowance was made for nights spent in taking cover from aeroplane bombs.

It was at this time that " Flu " introduced itself throughout the Battalion. Hardly anyone appeared immune to this epidemic. It raged in the Division from the Staff-Officer down to the Sanitary man and back again ; it made its appearance very suddenly, and was very severe whilst it lasted, but fortunately it was of short duration. There were a good number of cases in the Battalion, and a few victims had to be evacuated to the C.C.S. at Aire only to return again a few days afterwards.

There was a second " epidemic " almost immediately following " flu," and it originated in the carriage works at St. Venant. It was the epidemic of riding about in cabs, and usually only affected Transport Officers.

The generous Frenchman who owned the carriage works in St. Venant had left behind all sorts of vehicles of aristocratic appearance. There were ordinary closed cabs, the type used at weddings; landaus and Victorias, and so on. For a time it was considered the proper thing for Transport Officers of the Division, when taking up rations to their Battalions, to proceed by closed cab. An ordinary dog-cart, temporarily without an owner, was the most popular conveyance in the Battalion. This vehicle was duly reconstructed so as to render it suitable for G.S. harness. But it was feared that the owners of this wonderful chariot would in time recognise it, and in order to "break the ice" the Padre was sent out on his Sunday duties to visit the various Battalions under his spiritual care. Notwithstanding a prominent "dog collar" which the holy man wore, some fierce eyes and heated remarks were cast upon him by civilians who appeared to know the original owner. Subsequently the Padre refused the offer of riding in the cart, and borrowed a bicycle.

Eventually the owner himself turned up— complete with wife. Monsieur appeared to be a very harmless gentleman, but his wife . . . talked . . . screamed . . . swore . . . and used every abusive expression known and unknown in the French language.

The alterations carried out, which were admirable for G.S. harness, did not appear to meet the approval of Madame. But with the aid of some stout string the horse was tied between the shafts, and away the owners drove—man and wife, or rather let us say, wife and man. Madame for some unknown reason insisted on hoisting an umbrella, although there was no sign of rain—presumably it was an act of defiance towards the British Army in general. The outcome was an order received from Division to return all civilian vehicles to a dump, and heartbroken Transport Officers again took to saddles·

On the 31st May, the Battalion suffered the loss of Captain F. J. Blanchard, who was killed whilst in the sector. Blanchard had been with the Battalion from the earliest days, and besides being a competent Officer was very popular amongst all ranks—all who knew him felt his loss very keenly.

The Battalion was actually near St. Venant from April 11th to July 10th—three months, beginning with a terrific battle, and ending with a quiet front. Beyond the daily routine of pioneering, and construction of breastworks, life became rather dull.

On July 10th the Battalion moved to Blessy, a village about six kilos S.W. of Aire. At Blessy it stayed several days, and during this period Lieut.-Colonel H. Birchall, 1/7th D.L.I., joined as 2nd-in-Command. Colonel Birchall had commanded the 1/7th D.L.I., which was absorbed into another Durham Light Infantry Battalion. On relinquishing this command he came to the D.C.L.I., and remained with the 1/5th Battalion until after the Armistice.

After the Battalion had been at Blessy a few days, orders came through for a sudden move to the Hazebrouck sector, and the unit journeyed by 'bus to Staple, where a very limited number of billets were available—only a few scattered farms could be found. " A " Company had to bivouac in a field for several nights, and ultimately went further forward ' on detachment,' and carried out some pioneer work in the area near Hazebrouck.

At the beginning of August, 1918, the Germans began to evacuate the Merville salient which they found too costly to hold, and the Battalion which was then occupying huts in the Nieppe Forest (a familiar resort of the 1st Battalion, D.C.L.I.) had much work to carry out on forward roads and other tasks of this nature.

The situation on the German front never seemed quite clear, and occasionally it was found that they were still occupying certain positions which were reported as having passed into our hands.

" B " Company, of which Captain H. R. Trelawny was in command, received instructions to repair a piece of road between the edge of the Forest of Nieppe and Merville. 2nd Lieut. P. Malton carried out a reconnaisance of this work accompanied by a man of his platoon. They failed to return. 2nd Lieut. Robson, of the same Company, who went out in search of Malton, also failed to return. Later it transpired that Malton and his runner as well as Robson, had been captured by the Germans. 2nd Lieut Malton was unfortunately severely wounded in the leg, and died in Merville after an amputation. Robson escaped without injury, and was repatriated after the Armistice.

In the course of time the Battalion passed out of the Forêt de Nieppe, and occupied some shelters outside La Gorgue.

ONWARD, AUGUST TO
NOVEMBER, 1918

CHAPTER IX
Onward, August to November, 1918.

As the Germans retired the Pioneers moved farther afield, and it again fell to their lot to put in some very useful work, bridging, road making and repairing, etc. For this work the Battalion was specially commended by Major-General F. J. Duncan, Commanding the 61st Division, from whom was received the following message :—

" I have seen myself, and others have also noticed the excellent work done by your Officers and men during the recent advance. I have also a special word of praise for your N.C.O.'s, many of whom I have seen in command of parties doing real good work. The Pioneer is one of the most valuable men in the Service, with his assistance in consolidation, repair of roads, etc. Without him it would be well-nigh impossible to hold ground won. He must remember that he is also a fighting man. I have noticed with much pleasure the good spirit in your Battalion, and the hard work which is done, and I should be very glad if you would let all ranks know this."

Eventually the Battalion finished up in Estaires. The troops occupied at first the houses that remained standing in the town, but as mines were very prevalent, and H.V. shelling frequent, the majority of the Battalion moved to some Nissen huts and bivouacs just outside and N. of Estaires. " C " Company had several casualties owing to H.V. gunfire whilst in billets.

Estaires. Battalion H.Q. occupied the most pretentious house in the town—the Gas Works office, or manager's house, and for those who lived in this house there were many moments of excitement—ranging from the strained expectation of a mine explosion to some really good games of Badminton in the cinder-yard of the Gas Works. The German H.V. Gunners displayed a marked affection for this spot, and during most nights sprinkled shells somewhat freely round about.

Mines went up in most unexpected places, and on one occasion when the T.O. (Lieut. A. H. Paull) and Q.M. (Lieut. F. McAllister) were returning to the Transport lines, a portion of the main street disappeared into the air, about twenty yards ahead of them, resulting in a barrage of pavé.

Whilst at Estaires platoons had rest days in turn. The mornings of these days were spent

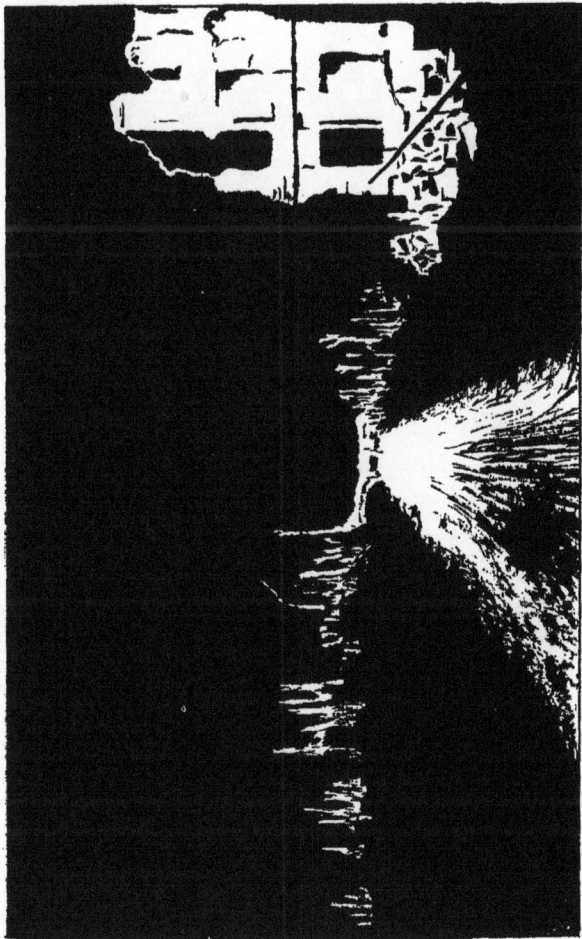

"It again fell to their lot to put in some very useful work, bridging, road making and repairing, etc."

This drawing, by E. C. Matthews, originally appeared in "The Veteran," May, 1921.

in general "cleaning up," and the afternoons
in small tactical schemes round the village. Trench
warfare had now practically disappeared, and it
was very necessary to practice these long-forgotten
tactics.

The Infantry of the Division was having a
strenuous time near Levantine towards the end of
September, and it was decided to withdraw the
Division from the line at the beginning of October.

On October 4th, the 1/5th D.C.L.I. moved
away from Estaires to a delightful village named
Bourecq, a few miles W. of Lillers. Here everyone
had excellent quarters.

After staying at Bourecq for several days
the Battalion moved down to the Cambrai area,
in order to take part in the final stages of the war.
The journey down was not too pleasant—one
very cold night was spent in the Hindenburg
line, which was now in British hands, but more
comfortable quarters were obtained in the Citadel
or College which was situated towards the villages
east of Cambrai.

On October 24th, the Battalion had a very
busy time during an attack by the 61st Division,
in the region of Montrecourt. It was necessary
to bridge certain streams in this vicinity, and

" A " Company was detailed for the operation. The actual bridging had to be repeated several times owing to direct hits of enemy shells on previously constructed bridges. In one instance a bridge was only just completed when it received a direct hit which completely destroyed it.

Lieut. Edwards of " A " Company carried out a great deal of very useful work in this direction, for which he received a bar to his M.C.

Sir Douglas Haig's Despatches of the March battle were published at the end of October, and the Battalion learned with jubilee that out of twelve Infantry Battalions mentioned the 1/5th D.C.L.I. was included.

The next morning a move was made to Haussy, but as that place was crowded out with troops, the Battalion was forced to move on through Saulzoir to St. Martin—a village adjoining Bermerain. The Germans had not left very long since. Their dead were still lying in and around the village. In some houses the clocks were tsill going, and articles of furniture were almost untouched, as the civilian inhabitants had either fled to the British lines, or travelled eastwards towards Mons.

Much work was done in order to place forward roads in such a condition that heavy guns and transport might pass along. Several times during the nights spent at St. Martin, the Battalion was subject to severe shelling. This " straffe " usually commenced when most of the troops were attempting to sleep, and ofttimes resulted in a desperate scramble for box respirators whilst half-asleep.

The lapse of War. An important piece of news came through whilst staying at St. Martin. The Turks had decided to cease their hostilities. Everyone was very braced with the prospect, and it was generally accepted that the Germans also would be seeking an Armistice. They were retiring very rapidly before the Allies' tremendous pressure beyond Cambrai.

General Debeney in his note stated :—" Our battle extended from the sea to the Moselle, on a 400 km. point, and 6,000,000 men were employed in it. Little wonder, therefore, that it lasted seven and a half months."

On Saturday, November 2nd, the 1/5th D.C.L.I. moved back to St. Aubert, and stayed there until November 4th, when it returned to St. Martin.

The Battalion earned from the Divisional Commander the following appreciation in a Special Order of the day on November 5th, 1918 :—

" The Division has indeed reason to be proud. I always knew you would do well, and I have often told you so, for I know well the fighting spirit in you all. From many outside sources I have heard of the excellent impression made by your smartness in turn-out, your readiness to salute, and your cheerfulness. Keep this up. Keep up the reputation you have earned. Keep up your fighting spirit. Be courteous to the inhabitants, and be thoughtful of their belongings. My warmest congratulations to you all. I am sure we shall march together to final victory. My best congratulations on your splendid work during the recent operations. You have done just as I expected the Duke of Cornwall's Light Infantry would do."

NAMUR AND THE HOME-COMING

M

CHAPTER X

Namur and the Home-Coming.

Then having "marched to final Victory," as signalised by the German acceptance of our peace terms, the Battalion received the following note from Major-General F. J. Duncan :—

Officers, N.C.O.'s and Men. On the conclusion of Peace, I wish to congratulate you on having so well upheld the traditions of the British Army during the trying period since the Armistice.

Brought together as most of you have been from many different units, I fully understand and sympathise with the difficult conditions under which you have been serving. These difficulties, however, you have overcome by discipline and goodwill. 'Whatever is worth doing is worth doing well,' and so you should keep up the old traditions of the British Army and the British race right up to the end for the sake of those who have given their lives to bring Peace and Freedom."

Demobilisation. After the Armistice the Battalion moved back to Cambrai, and from thence to Beaumetz. From Beaumetz it moved to Etaples, where it took over demobilisation work. Here men from other units joined, whilst many of the old soldiers of the Battalion were demobilised. The 1/5th D.C.L.I. next moved to Abancourt for the purpose of guarding dumps, and on July 21st it moved to Jambes in the Namur area.

When the Battalion left the 61st Division, it received a farewell letter from General Duncan, worded as follows :—

" The 1/5th Battalion, Duke of Cornwall's Light Infantry, has served in the 61st Division since April, 1916. It is now leaving. I part with the Battalion with very much regret. During its service in the 61st Division it has been known for its smartness, its efficiency, and its excellent discipline. It was further well known for its Pioneers, and as a fighting Battalion it has worthily upheld the reputation of its parent Battalions, the original Duke of Cornwall's Light Infantry. Although now made up of Officers and men of many different Regiments, the old spirit of the Battalion still lives on. May it continue to do so, and may the Battalion have Godspeed and good luck."

While in the Namur area, under canvas at Jambes, the Battalion spent a very pleasant time. Several cricket and football matches were played against local Army teams, and the Battalion also took part in a two-days' sports programme organised by Namur Area. The Battalion tug-of-war team won a competition after an exciting "final" against the Area Military Police. The M.P.'s were no match for the Battalion team, which simply "walked away" with them. During the summer months a steamer was on two occasions chartered for the day, and about 300 Officers, N.C.O.'s and men of the Battalion enjoyed a very pleasant river trip to Dinant, on the Meuse.

During October, at the request of the "Federation Nationale des Combattants," the Battalion sent Lieut. J. M. Tucker and a detachment of about 30 other ranks, to represent British troops in a celebration arranged by the "Section de Malonne." The following letter of thanks was received later from Monsieur Ledoux, the President of the Federation :—

"Monsieur le Commandant,

Nous avons l'honneur de vous adresser nos remerciments pour la participation de vos braves soldats a notre fete.

Tout le monde a admire la discipline, la correction et la belle attitude de la section que vous aviez bien voulu nous envoyer. Veuillez leur adresser l'espression de notre profounde gratitude et de notre admiration.

Daignez agreer, Monsieur le Commandant, l'assurance de nos sentiments repecteux."

From Namur Area the Battalion demobilised about 450 of its Officers and other ranks, and it then received orders to return once more to Etaples.

Here the Battalion was brought down to Cadre strength. The first anniversary of the Armistice Day was observed at Etaples by about 50 Officers and men of the Battalion, who stood to attention outside the Battalion Orderly Room for two minutes, in accordance with the special wish of His Majesty the King.

Back to Bodmin. On December 1st, the Cadre (Lieut.-Colonel E. B. Ward, Capt. G. F. Taylor, Lieut. and Quartermaster F. McAllister, and 35 other ranks) crossed to Dover, and on the following day the Officers, N.C.O.'s and men were welcomed back to their Territorial Depot at Bodmin by the Mayor, and Lieut.-Colonel W. A. Bawden who once again took command of the Battalion.

The Mayor (Mr. T. Hore), in welcoming the Cadre on behalf of his town and county, expressed the thanks of the inhabitants for what the Battalion had done for them. He hoped when the men settled down again into civil life they would feel the satisfaction of having done their duty as patriots on behalf of their King and Country.

Lieut.-Colonel Bawden was delighted to welcome the men to Bodmin, the home of the Battalion. Every movement had been followed with the greatest interest. It was not every Battalion that went away that had the honour of being mentioned by itself in despatches, but out of twelve Battalions in the whole of the British Army, the 1/5th D.C.L.I. was one of those mentioned. They were all very proud indeed that that Battalion had its Headquarters in Bodmin, and was a real Cornish Battalion. The deed for which it was recommended was that it held a very nasty piece of the line for 18 hours against the hordes of the German Army until relieved, losing nearly 300 men in so doing. When he (Col. Bawden) took the Battalion to France in 1916, practically all the men were from Cornwall. That showed how the County was linked around the 1/5th D.C.L.I. Every town, hamlet and village was interested in it, and when the History of the Regiment came to be written the 1st and 2nd parent Battalions would not be able to look back and say the 1/5th Battalion left them in the cart. That Battalion had done its duty, and it would be appreciated in later years. That day was a sad one for many who had lost their relatives in the conflict, but those men went out and did their duty, and the country was very proud of them.

Lieut.-Colonel Ward expressed the thanks not only of the Cadre, but the whole Battalion. It was perfectly true they had not such a large proportion of the original 1/5th Battalion now, as since the Armistice they had demobilised a large number, and had been augmented by men from other West-country Battalions. It was in no spirit of boasting, but he was very pleased and proud to know that the County of Cornwall had expressed its keen appreciation of the fact that the Battalion had been mentioned in despatches. It was a great pleasure to him to have the honour of commanding such a Battalion. He could not speak too highly of the way the Battalion had carried out its duties during the 20 months he had commanded it. Now that his last day with the Battalion had arrived, he desired to thank them all, not only for the way they had carried out the commands of the Officers, but also for the splendid way in which they had served their King and Country.

Following this a farewell letter was received from Colonel Ward :—

Farewell from Lieut.-Col. E. B. Ward. " Now that the services of the Battalion as a war Battalion have come to an end, and its members are scattered all over the country, and while many of us are in doubt as to what its future may be, I would like to write one last word of farewell, and of its past, which we remember so well.

To me the honour of being identified with such a Battalion, its associations, its spirit, the loyalty and devotion of all its members—Officers, W.O.'s, N.C.O.'s and Men—the sportsmanship and comradeship of all ranks, will always remain the most happy of memories. Coming to the Battalion at a time when it was shaken by heavy losses, its gallant leader killed, the situation dark and obscure, newly joined reinforcements flung in by the hundred, then on again to a fresh battlefield, still wider gaps in our ranks—scores of them mere boys, their first and only time in action—further reinforcements and many changes before the period of reorganisation set in ; I wish to thank all those who helped in that reorganisation and who set us on our feet again. But the spirit of the Battalion remained as ever, as it started and as it ended—if such spirit can ever end—and so down to the Armistice, and for over a year after. The process of demobilisation has been long and tortuous. Many have been the disappointments among those anxious to leave, and a few among those anxious to remain. Many have been the farewells, and many are the memories.

My very best wishes and thanks to you all. GOOD-BYE, GOOD LUCK AND GODSPEED."

A West of England newspaper, in reviewing the record of the 1/5th D.C.L.I. in the Great War, opened its remarks thus :—

" When all the stories have been told, and the war records of the many battalions of the British Army during the Great War have become history, the part played by the 1/5th Duke of Cornwall's Light Infantry will be found highly creditable to the battalion and to the county which it represents, and, in fact, worthy to stand side by side in the cold light of latter-day judgment with the records of battalions much better known before the war, and generally credited with greater exploits than the humble Pioneer Battalion from the far West country. But how many battalions can claim to have done their duty first as a pioneer unit, and then in a special emergency side by side with line battalions as a purely fighting unit, discarding the pick for the rifle ? Yet such is the record of the 1/5th D.C.L.I., and so thoroughly did they accomplish their new and unexpected task, that they were specially marked out for mention by Sir Douglas Haig in his despatch on the operations of March, 1918. That also is an honour which has fallen to few battalions during the present war, and it is a source of pardonable pride that it should have fallen to one which landed in France with 948 Cornishmen in its ranks out of a total strength of 999."

Thus endeth the human episode of a band of Pioneers in the struggles of a gigantic war. The exploits of the characters surpass any which romance might enfold. Yet one can only hope that sufficient copies will be read to overcome the cost of narration, despite the statement of Brig.-General the Hon. R. White, C.B., late

Commander of the 184th Infantry Brigade, that
" these Regimental Histories are the most valuable
of all contributions to the war histories. They
are free from the cheap sentiment of the
correspondent, and in most cases true pictures
of every day life in the Great War."

It would not be unreasonable to suppose
that, were the characters, incidents and scenes
of a Regimental History transformed into the
racy impossibilities of the fictitious, the first
and second editions would be swallowed on the
first day of publication by an absorbent public.
To-day many invaluable historical works, etc.,
are doomed to live or die in oblivion on account
of the tendency of the times by which Literature,
Music and Art seem to be guided. That Music
shares the same fate as Literature is shown
to be true by the ruthless neglect of the Opera
in favour of the light revue or musical comedy.
We look to Art and find a similar change, and so
on. It would appear that the public mind
has become divorced from the nobler themes
which for centuries past have directed and
inspired the British reading public. Let us hope,
however, that the decadence is only temporary,
and that the people will yet displace the sordid
and ephemeral, and again appeal for literature
of a edifying and permanent character.

RETROSPECT

RETROSPECT

The active war is over, but still there seems to be a silent tug-of-war going on between the nations of the world, behind the political curtain. However much there is in that idea of a " League of Nations " which Bernhardi describes as " a certain beautiful dream of nations living in peace side by side," human nature would see to it that there was another war.

Before August, 1914, the British people had allowed their myopia to gain possession of their common-sense. The Germans the whole time were plotting in the shadow, and the few statesmen and Generals who exposed the intrigues of these German agents, and who were calling upon the British people to arouse themselves, were targets of ridicule and aggression. Moreover, they were regarded as extravagant alarmists, and their propaganda a danger, rather than good sense. Most of us remember the unshakeable confidence our nation had in its security, and how afterwards we were so rudely awakened. Even in the darkest moments of the earlier part of the war, the stupidity of our false security led to a shortage of munitions, and the people at home wondered why the troops in France failed to do impossible things. It was only through the magnificent counter-action of Lloyd George, and the heroism and steadfastness of the British soldier, that we lived through those tragic days. No wonder that the war lasted so long. All these things are now history.

But are we again being lulled into a false security? War is still possible. As long as men remain men, force of war will determine the destiny of nations. Germany is still a menace, and I may be bold in saying that in this direction lies the seed of a greater war. Let us damn the idea of our living in peace side by side with the nations of the world, knit together by the red-tape of international convention, or the cultural principles of the League of Nations. Let us urge, rather, the rapid development of our martial powers. It will be far less expensive than another gruesome and drawn-out war. When peace was signed there were twenty-three wars going on. Although to a certain sect of people, construction of armaments is criminal and only catering for the worst in humanity, can we with safety and reason look on whilst other nations build big navies and raise huge armies ? What would become of the British Empire ? There is no suggestion of excess taxation or wasteful expenditure of public money—which might mean national ruin and bankruptcy, but it is a question of arterial importance that we should maintain our superiority. We are islanders, possessing a large mercantile marine which simply must be protected at all costs.

In a struggle of life and death, it is a question whether a nation can be entirely censured in introducing a weapon of human extermination not wholly justified by international convention. What steps are we taking to protect ourselves against probable development of scientific engines of war, such as the " Tank," or the introduction of likely novelties of chemical warfare, such as " Gas ? " Consider for a moment the horror felt at the brutal use of gas by the Germans, Had we kept pace with the evolution of modern warfare, or realized that international conventions were liable to be regarded as " scraps of paper," we might have saved thousands and thousands of lives. To join in a restricted compact in the future might jeopardise our national security, in addition to discouraging scientific research towards producing a superior weapon over our

N

enemies. If the latter were faced with the probability of new inventions of destruction unknown to them, this might be a step further in preventing future wars.

This is all very astounding to many after what has happened, but we are in the cockpit of fighting humanity. It would be tragic if now, having emerged more or less united, from one of the greatest of all trials, we resigned into apathy regarding the future. Events since the Armistice have proved that the danger exists. Are we going to encourage it ? If so, we are ignoring the great lesson of the war—that it is the nation and the Empire, not the individual, that counts.

The close of war brought with it many new aspects of our social life. Individuals of military bearing, sometimes in ill-fitting mufti, were to be seen wandering about in quest of work. They were referred to as " ex-Officers " and " ex-Service men," but as far as obtaining work was concerned some of them might have been ex-convicts. However, some really splendid assistance was given these men through the Officers' Association, the Comrades of the Great War, and the National Federation of Discharged and Demobilised Sailors and Soldiers, which three organisations later

(To face page 163)

The Profiteer's Visit to the Battlefields.

This cartoon, by E. C. Matthews, originally appeared in "The Granta," November 12th, 1920.

became amalgamated under the name of " The British Legion."*

At the same time, unfortunately, there were a number of men who, so long as charity maintained them, ceased to exert further efforts towards employment. Some ex-Officers, with eye-masks, would be seen daily in the metropolis turning the handle of barrel-organs, and so on. Not until Earl Haig made strong appeals on behalf of ex-Service men did matters improve.

The battlefields after the war proved to be just the thing to please those more or less useless people who, during the war, sent inspiring messages from their beds at home to old Tommy in the trenches :—" Cheer up, Tommy. Carry on. WE are all right." They were keeping alive that old traditional truth :—

When War is nigh, God and the Soldier is
the cry,
When War is o'er, and differences righted,
God is forgotten, and the Soldier slighted.

Numbers of these individuals are to-day making the battlefields an " excursion." They

* This formation comprised a body of three million men, who proved themselves the bulwark of Britain and the Empire, united by memories of " Keep the home fires burning," or " Tipperary," the " Bull Ring " at Rouen, the immortal Ypres Salient, the gay city of Cairo, the port of Bombay, or the sandy wastes of Mesopotamia.

gaze upon the sacred grounds of those past
familiar battle-haunts : Ypres, Merville, Arras,
St. Quentin, Albert, but they do not count the
number of wooden crosses which connect these
places, nor do they notice the silent wanderings
of a mother, or a father, in search of a grave.
They merely see the spectacular—the barbed
wire, the wrecked Tanks, the battered trenches,
the countless shell-holes, and so on. No wonder
poor Tommy sometimes wonders why he fought
for the old country.

At the end of 1920 the industrial and social
conditions of our country, and indeed the state of
the whole world, seemed very critical ; and to
emphasise the fact I cannot do better than quote
from an article of mine which appeared in the
Ex-Service Man at that time :—

"If an aviator hovering in the air above
England had the range of vision and observation
reaching around the globe, what would he see
to-day ? Looking below he would see masses
of the industrial world on 'strike,' at the same
time thousands and thousands of unemployed
men walking the streets in search of work.
Glancing towards the Emerald Isle he would
see the insurgency of the majority of the
Irish people. Gazing over districts of France,

Belgium, and Italy he would see the ghastly wounds of the late war, and the pathetic efforts of the inhabitants towards reconstruction. Farther afield he would trace the bloodstains of Bolshevism across Russia to the borders of Germany, and in Germany itself the smouldering ashes of a great militarism ready to be fanned into a threatening flame once again. Lastly, the desolation of Mesopotamia would attract his attention, and he would notice perhaps a little garrison holding out against the besieging onslaughts of the Arabs."

These were amongst the many aspects of post-war civilisation. Dissatisfaction was being fomented everywhere, especially permeating the labour classes, the country was confronted with innumerable strikes, and during all this the Irish trouble was growing to unknown magnitude. Reviewing these events, it is hoped that one can regard the majority of them in consequence of the war.

The nations of the world are more closely knit together by the advent of wireless telegraphy and aviation. Civilization and education have contributed to a fuller understanding and intercourse. Religion has been stamped on the world for hundreds of years. And yet . . . to-day we need not lift our eyebrows to see the sinister clouds of rivalry drifting this way, and drifting that way. When they clash we shall again hear the thunder of War.

For ourselves, the thread will hold the citizens of our huge Empire more firmly together, if the worthy traditions of our nationality are neither abused or neglected. Honour and justice demand that we carry on the immortal work of those who so gallantly sacrificed their lives in upholding our glorious heritage in times of national danger.

" We are the dead . . .
To you with failing hands we throw
The torch, be yours to lift it high.
If ye break faith with us who die
We shall not sleep, though poppies grow
In Flanders fields."

In almost every corner of the universe the familiar " red, white and blue " Union Jack flies over land where some British heroes lie, signalling a message such as that which rang out on that historic and fateful day of Trafalgar :

" ENGLAND EXPECTS THIS DAY THAT EVERY MAN
WILL DO HIS DUTY."

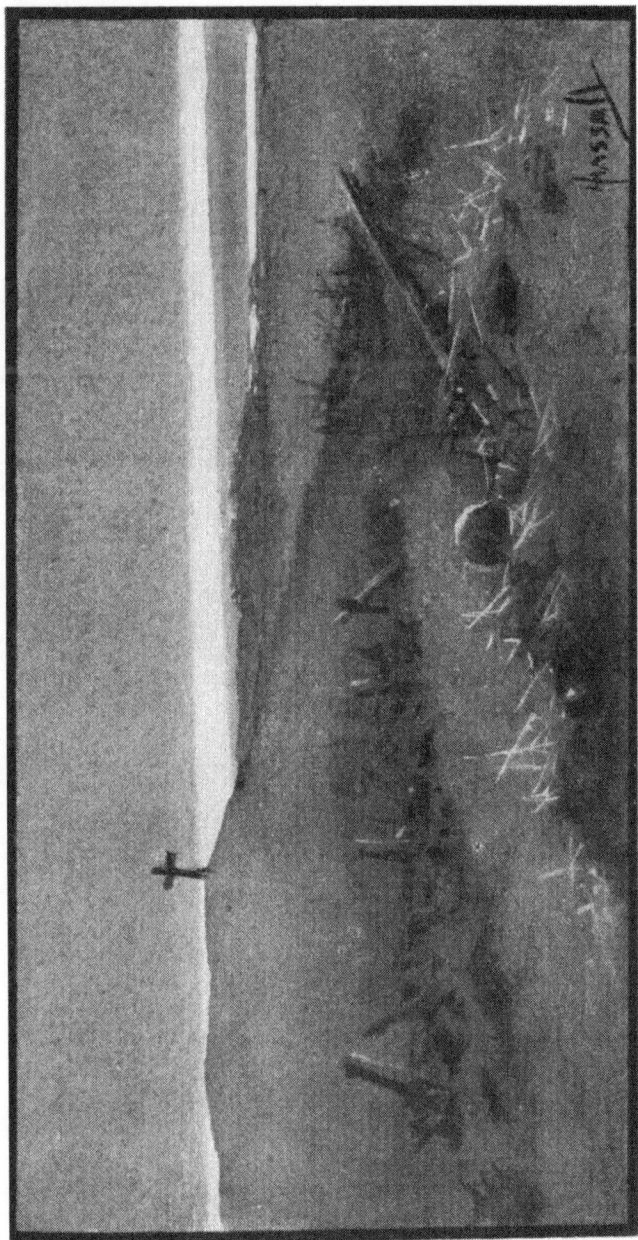

(To face page 166)

The End

Drawn by JOHN HASSALL, R.I.

Bibliography

WAR SERVICES OF THE 1/5TH BATTALION, DUKE OF CORNWALL'S
LIGHT INFANTRY, 1914–1919. Arranged by A. D. Chegwin.
1/5th D.C.L.I., Truro, 12/19. Price 9d. Proceeds in aid of
D.C.L.I. War Memorial. Publishers and Printers, Hiorns and
Miller, 107, Fore Street, Devonport.

THE STORY OF THE 2/4TH OXFORDSHIRE AND BUCKINGHAMSHIRE
LIGHT INFANTRY, by Captain G. K. Rose, M.C. With a Preface
by Brig.-General the Hon. R. White, C.B., C.M.G., D.S.O. (late
Commander 184th Infantry Brigade). Published by B. H.
Blackwell, Broad Street, Oxford. 1920.

THE OFFICIAL NAMES OF THE BATTLES AND OTHER ENGAGEMENTS
FOUGHT BY THE MILITARY FORCES OF THE BRITISH EMPIRE
DURING THE GREAT WAR, 1914-1919, AND THE THIRD AFGAN
WAR, 1919. Report of the Battles Nomenclature Committee
as approved by the Army Council. Published by His Majesty's
Stationery Office. 1921. Price 9d. net.

A SUBALTERN IN THE FIELD, by E. C. Matthews, Lieut. Duke of
Cornwall's Light Infantry. Illustrated from photographs taken
by the Author. Published by Heath, Cranton, Ltd., 6, Fleet
Lane, E.C.4, at 3s. 6d. net.

THE DUKE OF CORNWALL'S LIGHT INFANTRY. Official Copy. Printed
under the Authority of His Majesty's Stationery Office.

32ND FOOT. 1880. Notes on the History and Services of the Thirty-
second Regiment of Foot (Light Infantry).

WITH "THE THIRTY-SECOND" IN THE PENINSULAR AND OTHER
CAMPAIGNS, by Major Harry Ross-Lewin, of Ross Hill, Co. Clare.
Edited by John Wardell, M.A., Reader in Modern History in the
University of Dublin, and Professor of Jurisprudence and Political
Economy in the Queen's College, Galway. Dublin : Hodges,
Figgis & Co., Ltd., Publisher to the University. London :
Simpkin, Marshall & Co., Ltd. 1914.

HISTORICAL RECORD OF THE FORTY-SIXTH, OR THE SOUTH DEVONSHIRE, REGIMENT OF FOOT : containing an account of the formation of the Regiment in 1741 and of its subsequent . . . to 1851. Compiled by Richard Cannon, Esq., Adjutant-General's Office, Horse Guards. Illustrated with Plates. London : Parker, Furnivall & Parker, 30, Charing Cross, 1851.

HISTORICAL RECORDS OF THE 32ND (CORNWALL) LIGHT INFANTRY, now the 1st Battalion, Duke of Cornwall's L.I., from the formation of the Regiment in 1702 down to 1892. Compiled and edited by Colonel G. C. Swiney, from the Orderly Room Records and other sources. London : Simpkin, Marshall, Hamilton, Kent & Co., Limited, 32, Paternoster Row. Devonport : A. H. Swiss, 111 & 112, Fore Street. 1893.

OFFICERS DIED IN THE GREAT WAR, 1914-1919. Part I., Old and New Armies. Part II., Territorial Force. Published by His Majesty's Stationery Office. 1919. Price 7/6 net.

THE RED FEATHER. The Regimental Magazine of the 6th (Service) Battalion of the Duke of Cornwall's Light Infantry. Printed by Drew, Union Street, Aldershot.

THE QUARTERLY ARMY LIST. Part II. (War Services of Officers of the Army, etc.). January, 1921. Published by H.M.'s Stationery Office, Imperial House, Kingsway, London, W.C.2.

THE QUARTERLY ARMY LIST. April, 1921. Published by H.M.'s Stationery Office, Imperial House, Kingsway, W.C.2.

Who's Who, and Who was Who?
Biographical Notes.

"NOTE.—The bulk of the statements of service in connection with 'The War of 1914–20' are the personal statements only of individual officers, and do not constitute official recognition."—(From *The quarterly Army List*, Part II., January, 1921).

(T.) denotes service in the Territorial Force.

———————

CARUS-WILSON, T. (Lieut.-Colonel). An old Volunteer and Territorial and during the Boer War served in South Africa with the Composite Cyclist Corps. Had considerable experience of Lord Kitchener's blockhouse system, and was awarded the Queen's Medal with five clasps. On being mobilized in 1914, was at first engaged in guarding the Wireless Station at Poldhu. He was afterwards sent to India, where he served on the Viceroy's Guard of Honour. Returning to England in December, 1915, he was gazetted Major with the 1/5th Duke of Cornwall's Light Infantry and sailed with them to France in May, 1916. On January 11th, 1917, he assumed command of the Battalion, which had been relinquished by Lieut.-Colonel W. A. Bawden, owing to ill-health. This command he held up to the time of his death. He was three times mentioned in despatches, and was awarded the Territorial Decoration in December, 1917, and the Distinguished Service Order in March, 1918.

(T.) CHOMLEY, J. M. F. (Lt. 5 Bn. D. of Corn. L.I.). The War of 1914–9. M.C.

(T.) CHUDLEY, S. J. (Lt. 5 Bn. D. of Corn. L.I.). 1914–9. Empld. M.G.C. from 28 February, 1918. France and Belgium 17 April, 1916, to 11 November, 1918. Despatches, *Lond. Gaz.*, 18 December, 1917, and 9 July, 1919.

(T.) FIELD, E. E. (Lt. 5 Bn. D. of Corn. L.I.). The War of 1914–19. Despatches, *Lond. Gaz.*, 11 December, 1917, and 20 December, 1918. O.B.E.

(T.) HODGE, B. S. (Capt. 5 Bn. D. of Corn. L.I.). Operations in France and Belgium from 22 May, 1916, to 15 April, 1918. Wounded. Despatches, *Lond. Gaz.*, 22 May, 1917. M.C.

(T.) HODSON, E. M. (Capt. 5 Bn. D. of Corn. L.I.). Operations in France and Belgium from 22 May, 1916, to 16 April, 1918. Wounded. Despatches, *Lond. Gaz.*, 22 May, 1917.

(T.) JENNINGS, W. A. (Lt. 5 Bn. D. of Corn. L.I.). The War of 1914–9. Operations in France and Belgium from 15 November, 1915, to 2 March, 1916 ; from 17 November, 1917, to 12 December, 1917 ; from 3 April, 1918, to 11 November, 1918. Operations in Italy from 12 December, 1917, to 2 April, 1918. M.C.

(T.) JULYAN, WILLIAM L. (Lt. 4 Bn. D. of Corn. L.I.). Joined 5th Batt. in France as 2nd Lt., 18 June, 1917. Mentioned in despatches for services on Ypres front (Belgium), *Lond. Gaz.*, 7 November, 1917. Attached to 61st Divisional Staff from 1 September, 1917, to 26 October, 1918. Mentioned in Despatches for services on Merville front, *Lond. Gaz.*, 8 November, 1918. Appointed Acting Captain for duty as O.C. Divisional Employment Company and Salvage Officer, 61st Division, 26 October, 1918. Seconded Administrative Staff, 30 December, 1918, and appointed Deputy Assistant Director of Graves Registration and Enquiries, Third Army Area—Rank of Major, Class " BB." Appointed Assistant Director, Graves Registration and Enquiries, Third Army Area, 12th August, 1919. Rank of Lieut.-Col., Class " X " (as A.A.G.). Rejoined D.C.L.I. 8 March, 1920. Demobilized 8 March, 1920, with rank of Lieut.-Colonel, under A.O. 376 of 1918.

(T.) LEVERTON, L. S. (Lt. 5 Bn. D. of Corn. L.I.). The War of 1914–9. Wounded. Operations in France and Belgium from 22 May, 1916, to 9 April, 1918. M.C. Clasp to M.C.

MARRISON, C. C. Joined the 2/5th D.C.L.I. at Whitchurch, Tavistock, in July, 1915, as 2nd Lieutenant ; Lieutenant, July, 1916. After attending Pioneering Course at Reading proceeded overseas, October, 1916, and drafted to 7th D.C.L.I. Left the Battalion just before Christmas, and joined the 20th K.R.R. (Pioneers) on the Ancre. Moved to Arras later, and was wounded on March 2, 1917. Demobilized as Lieutenant, May, 1918.

MATTHEWS, ERNEST CHANNING. (Lt. ret. pay). (Lt. Unatt. List Terr. Force, Camb. Univ. Contgt. O.T.C., Senior Div.). Gazetted to 5th D.C.L.I. 27 August, 1915. Severely wounded as Lieut., 1st D.C.L.I., 28 June, 1918.

MEADOWS, G. S. (Lt.-Colonel). Proceeded to India on Oct. 9th, 1914, with the 1/4th (which was made up by amalgamation of the 4th and 5th Battalions, D.C.L.I. (T.F.) Served with the 1/4th in India, Aden and Palestine until July, 1917. Transferred to the 2/4th in India, August, 1917, and assumed command of the Battalion *vice* Col. P. Rogers, in May, 1918. Brought the 2/4th home for demobilization in December, 1919. Assumed command of the 5th Battalion on re-organization of the Territorial Force in March, 1920. O.B.E. (T.D.)

(T.) MILLETT, L. A. (Lt. 5 Bn. D. of Corn. L.I.). 1914–9. France and Belgium, June, 1916, to November, 1917. Egypt, September to December, 1915. M.C.

(T.) PARKER, W. F. (Maj. ret. pay). (Brev. Col. Terr. Force). 1914–20. Brev. of Col.

PLEYDELL-BOUVERIE, G. (Brev. Col. ret. pay). (Temp. Lt.-Col., 5 Bn. D. of Corn. L.I.). Egyptian Expedition, 1882. Action of Mahuta and Battle of Tele-l-Kebir. Medal with clasp ; Bronze Star. Bechuanaland Expedition, 1884–5. S. African War, 1901–2. Operations in Cape Colony, August, 1901, to 31 May, 1902. Queen's Medal with three clasps.

(T.) TREHANE, J. (Capt. 5 Bn. D. of Corn. L.I.). 1914–9. France and Belgium 21 May, 1916, to 11 November, 1918. Wounded. M.C.

WARD, E. B. (Maj. D. of Corn. L.I.). S. African War, 1899–1902. Operations in the Transvaal, March to 31 May, 1902. Queen's Medal with three clasps. King's Medal with two clasps. 1914–9. In command 10 (Serv.) Bn. D. of Corn. L.I. from 5 February, 1918, to 13 February, 1918. Afterwards in comd. of 5 Bn. D. of Corn. L.I., T.F., from 7 April, 1918, to 11 November, 1918. Operations in France and Belgium from 19 December, 1914, to 30 April, 1915 ; from 31 August, 1915, to 5 November, 1915 ; from 1 April, 1917, to 1 May, 1917 ; and from 12 October, 1917, to 11 November, 1918. Operations in Greek Macedonia, Serbia, Bulgaria, European Turkey, and the Islands of the Aegean Sea from 5 November, 1915, to 12 October, 1916. Despatches, *Lond. Gaz.*, 28 December, 1918, and 9 July, 1919. D.S.O.

(T.) WILLIAMS, F. (Capt. 5 Bn. D. of Corn. L.I.). 1914–9. Operations in France and Belgium from 22 May, 1916, to June, 1918. Despatches, *Lond. Gaz.*, 18 December, 1917.

ROLL OF HONOUR

Roll of Honour of Officers

Abbreviations :—k. in a. ... ... Killed in action.

              d. of w. ... ... Died of wounds.

              killed ... ... Killed, other than in action.

              died ... ... From natural causes, etc.

              p. ... ... Prisoner.

Abbreviations of Regiments and Battalions, enclosed in brackets after names, denote Officers attached.

Each Officer counted once only.

The 1/5th Battalion comprises 15 killed, 28 wounded, and 2 missing, making a total of 45.

Mr. Henry Charles Dickens, O.B.E., and others, have kindly assisted in compiling and arranging, but it is regretted that no assurance of accuracy can accompany the following details.

Attention is especially invited to the note in the " Preface " of the volume published by His Majesty's Stationery Office under the title *Officers Died in the Great War*, 1914–1919 :—

> " Nothing whatever contained in these rolls is to be quoted or made use of in any representation which it may be desired to make on the subject of rank, decoration, nature or date of casualty, or anything consequent upon any casualty."

The mere record of a Roll of Honour reveals nothing of the greatness of the sacrifice. To do full justice to the heroism of these Officers would be impossible, and to make a selection therefrom would be invidious. Nevertheless, it would be well for us all in scanning this roll, to remember the immortal lines of one of our soldier-poets, that—

> " There's some corner of a foreign field
> That is for ever England."

Killed in Action, Died of Wounds, Killed, or Died

Lieutenant-Colonel.

CARUS-WILSON, TREVOR, D.S.O., d. of w., 27/3/18.

Captain.

BALL, J., M.C., died 23/1/18. (1/D.C.L.I.).
BLANCHARD, FREDERICK JOHN, k. in a., 1/6/18.
TYACKE, CHARLES NOEL WALKER, k. in a., 23/3/18.

Lieutenant.

ALDERSON, ALEX GEORGE JERMYN, killed, 19/10/16. (And M.G.C.).
GOLDSWORTHY, THOMAS, k. in a., 12–14/4/18.
LORIMER, HUGH COWAN, died, 27/11/18.
MADDRELL, JOHN DENIS HUGH, d. of w., 13/12/16.
MORCOM, PERCIVAL JOHN HOSKING, k. in a., 11/4/18.
PALMER, HENRY JOHN, k. in a., 29/3/18.
SMITH, LEON WALTER, k. in a., 12/4/18. (4/D.C.L.I.).
THOMAS, FRANCIS BERNARD VIVIAN, k. in a., 22/9/16. (4/D.C.L.I.).

Second Lieutenant.

BEER, LEWIS CHARLES, k. in a., 28/3/18.
BISHOP, BERNARD BENNETT, k. in a., 9/9/17. (Attd. R.F.C.).
BLACKMORE, EDWIN, k. in a., 16/8/16. (And M.G.C.).
BRETT, ERNEST HUGH WILLIAM, d. of w., 2/8/16. (Temp. 2/Lt., 9/D.C.L.I.).
CHAPPLE, REGINALD CHARLES, k. in a., 12/4/18. (4/D.C.L.I.).
COOMBE, LESLIE CLARENCE, k. in a., 25/3/18. (Temp. 2/Lt., 1/D.C.L.I.).
EVERSON, CHARLES PERCY, k. in a., 7/10/16.
(p.) MALTON, PAUL LOCOCK, d. of w., 3/9/18. (1/D.C.L.I.).
MITCHELL, HENRY WILLIAM, k. in a., 22/11/17.
MITCHELL, TERENCE HARGREAVES, d. of w., 6/11/16.
MORCOM, FRANK CLIFFORD, k. in a., 8/5/17.
RATCLIFF-GAYLAND, ERIC RONALD, k. in a., 20/7/16.
ROWSE, RICHARD SIDNEY, died, 2/9/15.

Wounded, Wounded and Missing, or Wounded and Prisoner

Captain.

HODGE, B. S., M.C.
HODSON, E. M.
JEFFERY, W. A.
POTTER, W. E.
WOOD, T. A. V.

Lieutenant.

CHOMLEY, J. M. F.
DIXON, C. D.
GEACH, R. D.
GREEN, A.
HUGHES, A. G.
LORIMER, H. C.
LEVERTON, L. S.
MARRISON, C. C.
O'CARROLL, G. C. W.   (4/D.C.L.I.).
(p.) RICKARD, H.
ROSS, H. E.
TAYLOR, W. H.
TREHANE, J.
TRELAWNY, H. R.

Second Lieutenant.

AEDY, E. C.
(p.) BLACKLOCK, H. A.
CAINE, J. H.
DREWETT, W. J.
HUGHES, C. E. C.
HUNT, R. G.
LUSCOMBE, R. A.
NEWBOULT, A. T.   (1/D.C.L.I.).
RYDE, W. H.
SMITH, W. F.   (4/D.C.L.I.).
TREWBELLA, H. R.
VOWLES, C. E.
WARD, F. S.
YELF, F. W.

List of Officer Casualties from November, 1916, to November, 1918

November, 1916.

Lieut. J. D. H. Maddrell, died from wounds received on the Somme.
Capt. T. A. V. Wood, wounded on the Somme.

December, 1916.

Capt. J. Trehain, M.C. ,, ,, ,,

June, 1917.

2nd Lieut. C. E. Vowles, ,, at Arras.

December, 1917.

Lieut. Dixon, ,, at Cambrai.

March, 1918.

Lt.-Col. T. Carus-Wilson, killed in the Battle of St. Quentin.
Capt. C. W. N. Tyacke, ,, ,, ,, ,,
Lieut. H. J. Palmer, ,, ,, ,, ,,
2nd Lieut. L. C. Beer, ,, ,, ,, ,,
2nd Lieut. L. C. Coombe, ,, ,, ,, ,,
Capt. W. E. Potter, Adjt., wounded in the Battle of St. Quentin.
Lieut. A. G. Hughes, Asst. Adjt., ,, ,, ,, ,,
Capt. W. Jeffery, ,, ,, ,, ,,
Lieut. L. S. Leverton, ,, ,, ,, ,,
Lieut. H. C. Lorimer, ,, ,, ,, ,,
Lieut. J. F. Chomley, ,, ,, ,, ,,
Lieut. W. Taylor, ,, ,, ,, ,,
Lieut. H. E. Ross, ,, ,, ,, ,,
2nd Lieut. R. Chapple, ,, ,, ,, ,,
Capt. F. Blanchard, ,, ,, ,, ,,

April, 1918.

Lieut. T. Goldsworthy, killed in the Merville operations.
Lieut. W. Smith, ,, ,, ,, ,,
Lieut. P. J. Morcom, ,, ,, ,, ,,
2nd Lieut. R. Chapple, ,, ,, ,, ,,
Capt. E. M. Hodson, wounded in the Merville operations.
Capt. Brian S. Hodge, ,, ,, ,, ,,
Lieut. H. R. Trelawny, ,, ,, ,, ,,
2nd Lieut. C. E. C. Hughes, ,, ,, ,, ,,
2nd Lieut. Green, ,, ,, ,, ,,
2nd Lieut. G. C. O'Carroll, ,, ,, ,, ,,
2nd Lieut. W. F. Smith, ,, ,, ,, ,,

Date of Casualty unknown.

2nd Lieut. Aedy.
2nd Lieut. W. G. Hunt.
2nd Lieut. Drewitt.

2nd Lieut. H. Blacklock was taken prisoner in the Merville operations, 1918.
Lieut. H. C. Lorimer died whilst at Hospital in England, early 1919.
Capt. J. F. Blanchard was killed in the Merville Sector, 31st May, 1918.

August, 1918.

2nd Lieut. Robson, was taken prisoner in the Merville Sector.
2nd Lieut. Paul Malton,* ,, ,, ,, ,, ,,

---

* Discovered later that 2nd Lieut. Paul Malton died whilst a prisoner in German hands after having a leg amputated.

APPENDIX

APPENDIX

DECORATIONS

LIEUT.-COLONEL T. CARUS-WILSON ... ... D.S.O. Feb., 1918.
LIEUT.-COLONEL E. B. WARD ... ... D.S.O. June (?) 1919.
MAJOR B. S. HODGE (then Capt. O.C. "C" Coy.) M.C. April, 1918.
LIEUT. L. S. LEVERTON (D. and A. Coys.) ... M.C. August, 1917.
Bar March, 1918.

LEVERTON, L. S., 2nd Lt., D. of Cornwall's L.I. (T.) ;
October 18th, 1917 ; Bar to M.C., September 16th, 1918 :—" For
conspicuous gallantry and devotion to duty in reconnoitring
and establishing a machine-gun position in unknown country
in the dark. During the night he was subjected to intense
gas shelling. Though 22 of his 25 men were sent to hospital
on their return the work of consolidation went on."

" When in temporary command of a company he successfully organised his defence under heavy fire, and secured his
flank against enemy attacks. He withdrew his men with great
skill, constantly checking the enemy and stubbornly contesting
all ground. Later, he showed the utmost disregard for his
personal safety, rescuing wounded men on several occasions
under heavy fire. His example throughout was an inspiration
to all ranks." (M.C. gazetted October 18th, 1917).

LIEUT. F. SOWARD (D. Coy. and "C") ... M.C. August, 1917.
CAPT. J. TREHANE (A and B Coy.) ... ... M.C. April, 1918.
LIEUT. EDWARDS (A Coy.) ... ... M.C. April, 1918.
Bar October, 1918.
LIEUT. J. F. CHOMLEY (B Coy.) ... ... M.C. March, 1918.
LIEUT. A. H. PAULL (T.O.) ... ... M.C. Dec., 1918.
LIEUT. E. C. DAVIES (A Coy.) ... ... M.C. June (?), 1919.

AWARDED TO AN OFFICER WHILST ATTACHED TO THE 7TH D.C.L.I.

LIEUT. (Actg. Capt.) T. W. WATERS, 5th (attd. 7th) D.C.L.I. ... M.C.
At Acheville, on the night of Sept. 26-27, 1918, in
command of his company, he displayed splendid dash in
leading his troops close up under our barrage to the enemy
trench. He was first to reach the trench, and, jumping in
shot several of the enemy. When the enemy made a strong
counter-attack on the night of the 27th, he showed great
initiative in maintaining touch with the battalion on the right,
and throughout the night he showed great courage and devotion
to duty.

Medical Officers associated with the 1/5th D.C.L.I. during its Great War existence :—

LIEUT. —. WOOD, R.A.M.C.	Feb., 1917.
CAPTAIN R. C. COATSWORTH, M.C., (R.A.M.C.)...	March, 1918.
LIEUT. H. E. THOMPSON, R.A.M.C.	April 18 to Feb., 1919.

Padres (C. of E.) :—

The REV. —. WINTER ...	Somme, Nov., 1916, to Feb., 1917.
The REV. —. STAVELEY...	Feb., 1917, to April, 1917.
The REV. —. BELL ...	April, 1917, to July, 1917.
The REV. P. C. T. CRICK (Sen. Chaplain 61st Div.)	July, 1917, to Sept., 1917.
The REV. —. SHIELDS ...	Sept., 1917 (?)

Commanding Officers :—

England ... LIEUT.-COL. PLEYDELL BOUVERIE.
    LIEUT.-COL. PARKER.
    LIEUT.-COL. BAWDEN.

France ... LIEUT.-COL. BAWDEN, T.D. December, 1916.
    LIEUT.-COL. T. CARUS-WILSON, D.S.O. Dec., 1916. to March, 1918. (Killed in action, March 25, 1918).
    LIEUT.-COL. E. B. WARD, D.S.O. April, 1918, to November, 1919 (?)

Adjutants :—

France ... CAPTAIN J. BALL, M.C. May, 1916, to April, 1917. (Evacuated to England (sick). Died in hospital in London, February, 1918.)

    CAPTAIN W. F. POTTER. April, 1917, to March, 1918. (Wounded St. Quentin battle, returned to duty after having wound dressed, but later was evacuated to England.)

    CAPTAIN J. TREHANE, M.C. April, 1918, to October, 1918. (Acting Adjutant.)

    CAPTAIN G. F. TAYLOR. October, 1918, to November, 1919.

(*From the " Army List, March*, 1921.")

THE DUKE OF CORNWALL'S LIGHT INFANTRY—(Regtl. Dist. No. 32.)
5TH BATTALION (TERRITORIAL.)
" SOUTH AFRICA, 1900-01."
THE DRILL HALL, BODMIN.

Hon. Colonel.

POLE-CAREW, Hon., Lt.-Gen. Sir R., K.C.B.,
    C.V.O. (R), ret. pay, Col. D.C.L.I. ...   13 Jan., 1909.

In Command (temp.)

BAWDEN, W. A., TD, Lt.-Col. late T.F. Res. ...   16 Aug., 1919.

Lt.-Colonels.

EDYVEAN, R. C. F. ... ...   27 March, 1918.
MEADOWS, G. S., TD (*In command*) ... ... O.B.E. 16 Feb., 1920.

Majors.

HODGE, B. S. ... ... M.C. 27 March, 1918.

Captains.

STEWART, M. J. (q) (*H*) ... ...   25 June, 1914.
WILLIAMS, F. ... ...   26 Sept., 1914.
HAUGHTON, A. L., Adjt. ... ...   19 Dec., 1914.
THOMAS, J. A. ... ...   2 April, 1916.
MARTIN, H. S. ... ...   1 June, 1916.
HODSON, E. M. ... ...   1 June, 1916.
GILCHRIST, H. ... ...   1 July, 1916.
PARKER, J. L. ... ...   10 Nov., 1917.
BAWDEN, A. J. F. ... ...   17 Nov., 1917.
TREHANE, J. ... ... M.C. 23 March, 1918.
PETHERICK, D. M. ... ...   27 April, 1918.
PHILLIPS, R. F. ... ... M.C. 1 July, 1918.
STONEMAN, H.... ... ... M.C. 18 June, 1920.

Lieutenants.

MOULD, W. (*Empld. A.E.C.*) ... ...   1 June, 1916.
CHOMLEY, J. M. F. ... ... M.C. 27 Jan., 1917.
GEACH, P. ... ...   1 July, 1917.
PRISK, J. M. ... ...   1 July, 1917.
GARLAND, P. H. ... ...   1 July, 1917.
MABBOTT, H. V. ... ...   1 July, 1917.
LEVERTON, L. S. ... ... M.C. 1 July, 1917.
ROSS, H. E. ... ...   1 July, 1917.
WATERS, T. W. ... ... M.C. 1 July, 1917.

CLAYTON, N. J. H.		1 July, 1917.
DINGLE, P. J.		1 July, 1917.
HILL, R. F.		1 July, 1917.
CRAZE, F.		1 July, 1917.
BAWDEN, F. M. M.		1 July, 1917.
PAULL, A. H.	M.C.	1 July, 1917.
HAINSSELIN, S.		1 July, 1917.
WILLIAMSON, A. S.		1 July, 1917.
BOUNDY, P. M., o.d.		1 July, 1917.
MACFARLANE, A. A.		1 July, 1917.
MERRICKS, L. M.		1 July, 1917.
PENGELLY, T. W. R.		1 July, 1917.
CHUDLEY, S. J.		1 July, 1917.
DAVIES, E. C.	M.C.	1 July, 1917.
MARTIN, T.		1 July, 1917.
WILLIAMS, L. J., i.r.		1 July, 1917.
ROGERS, W. E.		1 July, 1917.
FIELD, E. E. (*Lt. R.E.)	O.B.E.	1 July, 1917.
WILLCOCK, F. E.		1 July, 1917.
HARRIS, H. A.		1 July, 1917.
CATER, W. L.		1 July, 1917.
MILLETT, L. A.	M.C.	1 July, 1917.
TAYLOR, W. H.		1 July, 1917.
UREN, S. G. G.		15 July, 1917.
SOWARD, F.	M.C.	15 July, 1917.
FARRIER, A. V., f.c.		16 July, 1917.
HODGE, W. E.		31 Jan., 1918.
WILLS, E.		26 March, 1918.
POTTER, W. E.		8 July, 1918.
JENNINGS, W. A.	M.C.	1 Feb., 1919.
HUGHES, C. E. C.		3 Feb., 1919.
LUSCOMBE, R. A.		3 Feb., 1919.
MUTTON, N.		18 June, 1919.
GUY, J. S.		13 Sept., 1919.
MARKS, H. E.	M.B.E.	18 October, 1919.
CHIVERS, F. S.		1 Nov., 1919.
GOLLEDGE, A.		1 Nov., 1919.
FISHER, S.		1 Nov., 1919.
BIBBINGS, W. E.		29 Nov., 1919.
PERKS, E. J.		29 Nov., 1919.
PASCOE, J. J.		1 March, 1920.
		1 July, 1917.

PALMER, C. C. R. ... ... 1 March, 1920.
HURRELL, H. ... ... 1 March, 1920.
ELLIS, W. V. H. ... ... 1 May, 1920.
JANE, P. ... ... 4 August, 1920.
26 October, 1918.

2nd Lieutenants.

KING, T. F. ... ... 23 Nov., 1918.
KNAPP, E. A. ... ... 1 May, 1918.
PAGE, J. O. ... ... 1 May, 1918.
IVORY, C. A. ... ... 1 March, 1920.
DINGLEY, J. ... ... 18 August, 1920.

Adjutant.

HOUGHTON, A. L., *capt.* ... ... 12 March, 1920.

Quarter-Master.

STEAR, B. T., *capt.* ... ... 10 May, 1920.
12 Sept., 1918.
McALLISTER, F., *lt.* ... ... 18 April, 1918.

Chaplain.

BROWNE, REV. L., M.A., Chapl. 4th Class
R.A. Ch. D. (T.F.) (*attd.*) ... ... 29 May, 1913.

(Uniform—*Scarlet.* Facings—*White.*)

CADET UNIT AFFILIATED.

CHURCH LOYALTY GUARDS, " G " Co., 1st Cadet Bn. of Cornwall.
* Temporary.

TERRITORIAL FORCE RESERVE.
THE DUKE OF CORNWALL'S LIGHT INFANTRY.
5th Battalion.

Maj. ... WHITFORD, C. E., TD ... ... 10 Nov., 1914.
Maj. ... EDYVEAN, M. F., TD, *p.c.* ... 2 April, 1916.
Maj. ... TROOD, F. T. ... ... 27 March, 1918.
Capt. ... GEACH, R. D. ... ... 22 Dec., 1918.
Capt. ... McNALY, J. ... ... 24 August, 1919.
Lt. ... DOUGLASS, F. ... ... 28 Dec., 1914.

4th Battalion. (*Territorial.*)
Lieutenants.

(5) POOLE, A. L. ... ... 1 July, 1917.
(5) DREWETT, W. J. ... ... 28 May, 1919.

TERRITORIAL FORCE ASSOCIATION.
CORNWALL.

President.
WILLIAMS, J. C., Esq. (*Lord Lieutenant.*)
Chairman.
VYVYAN, Col. Sir C. B., Bt., C.B., C.M.G., D.L., ret. pay, *p.s.c.*
Vice-Chairman.
FOSTER, Col. L. C., VD, D.L., late 2 V.B. D. of Corn. L.I.
Military Members.
BAWDEN, Lt.-Col. W. A., TD, 5 Bn. D.C.L.I.
CHELLEW, Maj. T. J., O.B.E., TD, R.G.A. (T.F.)
FOSTER, Col. L. C., VD, D.L., late 2 V.B. D. of Corn. L.I. (*Vice-Chairman*).
GRAHAM, Capt. H. S., Fort. R.E. (T.F.)
JEFFERY, Col. J., VD, late 4 Bn. D. of Corn. L.I.
LOVERING, Lt.-Col. W. T., VD, late 1 Corn. V.A.
MARSACK, Col. E. L., O.B.E., VD, late 5 Bn. D. of Corn. L.I.
MEADOWS, Lt.-Col. G. S., O.B.E., TD, 5 Bn. D.C.L.I.
OATS, Lt.-Col. F. F., TD, R.G.A. (T.F.)
ST. LEVAN, Brig.-Gen. J. T., Lord, C.B., C.V.O., Corn. R.G.A. (Col. ret. pay).
SMITH, Lt.-Col. G. E. S., D.S.O., TD, 4 Bn. D.C.L.I.
SMITH, Col. Sir G. J., Knt., VD, 4 Bn. D.C.L.I.
VIVIAN, Maj. G. C. B., Lord, D.S.O., TD, R. 1 Devon. Yeo.
Representative Members.
County Council.
BAIN, F. D., Esq., J.P.
GRYLLS, T. R., Esq., J.P.
Co-opted Members.
CARKEEK, Sir A., Knt., J.P.
FORD, Maj. J. A., R.E. (T.F.)
POLWHELE, A. C., Esq.
POOLE, Maj.-Gen. Sir F. C., K.B.E., C.B., C.M.G., D.S.O., ret. pay.
RICHARDS, C. J., Esq.
ROBERTS, Lt.-Col. J. D. A., J.P., late Res. of Off.
ST. GERMANS, Capt. J. G. C., Earl of, M.C., Res. of Off.
THOMAS, C. V., Esq.
VYVYAN, Col. Sir C. B., Bt., C.B., C.M.G., D.L., ret. pay *p.c.c.* (*Chairman*).
WILLIAMS, Maj. G. T., Res. of Off.
Secretary.
HOOD, Lt.-Col. Hon. N. A., C.M.G., D.S.O., ret. pay (Res. of Off.), The Armoury, Pydar Street, Truro. (Regd. tel. address " Associate," Truro.)
UNITS ADMINISTERED BY THE ASSOCIATION.
Royal Artillery.
Corn. R.G.A. (5 Cos., 2 Heavy Batts.)
Royal Engineers.
Corn. Fort.
Infantry.
4 & 5 Bns. D.C.L.I.

INDEX